T0334810

The People Are Missing

SERIES EDITORS · *Marco Abel and Roland Végső*

PROV
OCAT
IONS

Something in the world forces us to think.
—Gilles Deleuze

The world provokes thought. Thinking is nothing but
the human response to this provocation. Thus, the very
nature of thought is to be the product of a provocation.
This is why a genuine act of provocation cannot be the
empty rhetorical gesture of the contrarian. It must be
an experimental response to the historical necessity to
act. Unlike the contrarian, we refuse to reduce provocation to a passive noun or a state of being. We believe
that real moments of provocation are constituted by
a series of actions that are best defined by verbs or
even infinitives—verbs in a modality of potentiality,
of the promise of action. To provoke is to intervene
in the present by invoking an as yet undecided future
radically different from what is declared to be possible
in the present and, in so doing, to arouse the desire
for bringing about change. By publishing short books
from multiple disciplinary perspectives that are closer
to the genres of the manifesto, the polemical essay,
the intervention, and the pamphlet than to traditional
scholarly monographs, "Provocations" hopes to serve
as a forum for the kind of theoretical experimentation
that we consider to be the very essence of thought.

www.provocationsbooks.com

The People Are Missing

Minor Literature Today

GREGG LAMBERT

UNIVERSITY OF NEBRASKA PRESS · LINCOLN

Portions of this manuscript were first
published in Czech in *Gilles Deleuze o
literatuře: Mezi uměním, animalitou a politikou*,
by Michaela Fišerová, Martin Charvát,
and Gregg Lambert (Prague: Metropolitan
University Prague Press, 2019).

The series editors would like to thank
Luke Folk, Anne Nagel, Robert
Lipscomb, and Joseph Turner for
their work on the manuscript.

Library of Congress
Cataloging-in-Publication Data
Names: Lambert, Gregg, author.
Title: The people are missing: minor
literature today / Gregg Lambert.
Description: Lincoln: University of Nebraska
Press, [2021] | Series: Provocations |
Includes bibliographical references.
Identifiers: LCCN 2020025021
ISBN 9781496224316 (paperback)
ISBN 9781496225672 (epub)
ISBN 9781496225689 (mobi)
ISBN 9781496225696 (pdf)
Subjects: LCSH: Literature—Philosophy—
History—20th century. |
Literature—Philosophy—History—
21st century. | Criticism.
Classification: LCC PN45 .L31625
2021 | DDC 801—dc23
LC record available at
https://lccn.loc.gov/2020025021

Set in Sorts Mill Goudy by Laura Buis.
Designed by N. Putens.

CONTENTS

PROVOCATIONS

Year 0—The Refrain "The People Are Missing"

Why did Deleuze essentially abandon the hope for the revolutionary goals of "minor literature" or a "minor cinema" between 1975 (the publication with Félix Guattari of *Kafka: Toward a Minor Literature*) and 1985 (the publication of *Cinema 2*)? Even though he continues to invoke the refrain "the people are missing" as the ultimate justification of the revolutionary potential of the artwork as an act of resistance against the various forms of majority, the sense of the refrain itself undergoes an evolution from revolutionary aspiration of an existing minor people to a millenarian and eschatological hope for a "people to come." Was the cause of this change the external conditions of the artwork in the coming age of neoliberalism? Or, was it the discovery of an error in the transcendental deduction of the symbolic analogy between aesthetics and politics, which dominates Deleuze's earlier works of philosophy (especially *Difference and Repetition*)? If the latter, then the hope of deducing the passage between the aesthetic act and the act of politics is unfounded, and the major program of political interpretation that has dominated the field of aesthetics for the last fifty years can now be proven to be in default. It follows that we must abandon the political interpretation of the artwork as a dead end and invent an entirely new aesthetic discipline in order to understand the real conditions of art and literature, or whatever forms of the imagination are emerging today to replace these historical genera. This does necessarily mean that interpretation becomes "nonpolitical" (purely aesthetic or formalist), and we must reject this blackmail that has maintained the hegemony of the tribunal of political interpretation in the academy for the past three decades. In fact, today we still have no clear understanding of the ideal genesis whereby the act of imagination provides a "passage" to the practical field of action, creating in the practical subject the intensity of a feeling for the universal aspirations of any politics still worthy of the name.

The major provocations that follow from this hypothesis are as follows:

- The regime of political interpretation is a dead end and has lost or obscured the real conditions of minority creation, if not the act of creation itself.
- The long divorce between the creative writing faculty and the critical faculty in the contemporary university has resulted in a fractured vocation of "literature" today.
- "Literary history" is a major tautology that alienates the power of the imagination and the act of creation to the past, outside the present where the real situation of minor writing still exists.
- It is obvious that the entire question of literature today, including so-called minor literature, is no longer the concern of any "people," either living or dead.
- The power of art or literature may indeed invoke the presence of an absent or missing people, but it cannot invent them.

- As a result, what is called "minor literature" only exists today in universities, and "the people" have become, according to Deleuze and Guattari's premonition, merely "a cardboard or paper people."
- In place of a majoritarian institution of literary history, the publishing regime of contemporary literature, the creative writing workshop, and the literary prize have become factories for producing "outstanding talent" and "major authors," and the criterion of natural genius becomes an object of discipline and commercial marketing.
- In order to liberate the concept of "minor literature" today, the first thing we do, let's kill all the critics, and second, close all the creative writing factories.

The People Are Missing

1

The Axiom of Political Interpretation

"The people are missing" (*Le peuple manque*) is a constant refrain in Gilles Deleuze and Félix Guattari's writings after the 1975 publication of *Kafka: Pour une litterature mineure*. With the translation of this work into English in 1986, the refrain quickly became a hallmark of political interpretation in the North American academy and was especially applied to the works of minorities and postcolonial writers. However, in the second cinema book, which appeared ten years later, *Cinéma 2: L'Image-temps*, the refrain was restricted to the conditions of third-world cinema, especially the decline or breakup of the classical period of the mass art form along with the national vocation that had been assigned to it throughout the prewar period, particularly in the national cinemas of the United States and the Soviet Union. According to Deleuze, it is now only the cinema of "third-world directors" such as Carmello Bene and Jean-Louis Comolli, but also of French and German directors such as Alain Resnais and Jean Marie Straub, that defines the conditions of a truly postwar political cinema: the absence, even the impossibility, of a people who would constitute its organic community. In a nutshell, this will become the basic theme of *Cinema 2*, which depicts this period of postwar cinema. As Deleuze concludes in 1985:

It is as if modern political cinema were no longer constituted on the basis of a possibility of evolution and revolution, like the classical cinema, but on impossibilities, in the style of Kafka: *the intolerable*. Western authors cannot save themselves from this impasse, unless they settle for a cardboard people and paper revolutionaries: it is a condition which makes Comolli a true political film-maker when he takes as his object a double impossibility, that of forming a group *and* that of not forming a group, "the impossibility of escaping from the group and the impossibility of being satisfied with it" (*L'ombre rouge*).

If the people are missing, if there is no longer consciousness, evolution or revolution, it is the scheme of reversal which itself becomes impossible. There will no longer be conquest of power by a proletariat, or by a united or unified people.[1]

Consequently, one of the motives for the following reflections on the concept of "minor literature" is simply to ask what had changed in the period between the two works to narrow the earlier definition of "becoming minor." I will return later to Deleuze's writings on cinema from the mid-1980s to explore whether the same conditions identified with this political cinema still exist today, or whether any reference to the art form has become partly nostalgic and utopian—perhaps beginning in the period of Deleuze's own analysis, which already foreshadows the decline of the auteur function and, in its place, the somewhat nebulous collective enunciation of what he calls, following Paul Klee, "anonymous mediators." Given the small number of directors upon whom Deleuze bases his analysis and the fact that most of them were either published in or associated with the French journal *Cahiers du Cinéma* after 1963—when Jacques Rivette replaced Eric Rohmer as editor in chief and the journal emphasized global cinema and a Jacobean style of Maoist revolutionary politics—we might speculate that this cinema achieved its high point in the mid-1970s, before it also began to decline as a dominant style of political cinema. Deleuze also refers to the conditions found in black American cinema of the 1970s, although his reference is nonspecific and does not exemplify any particular films or directors.[2]

Since my reflections on the evolution of the sense of the refrain are not principally concerned with the periodization of the political cinemas of the "third world"—a term that already betrays an outdated political rhetoric!—I will analyze the philosophical and aesthetic assumptions that underlie the refrain itself. The two primarily modernist sources for this refrain are well known, namely, Franz Kafka and Paul Klee. More specifically, the first component of the refrain is taken from Kafka's five-page diary entries of 1911 on the literature of a small nation concerning the situation of the Czech writer in the breakup of the Habsburg Monarchy and the fragmentary or "patchwork" character of collective enunciation in the absence of a national literary history. Klee provides the second component of the refrain in his 1924 lecture on the difficulty of creating art in the absence of a community that carries him. He describes his dream for "a work of vast scope," a "Great Work": "We have found its parts, but not yet the whole. This last force is lacking for want of a people that carries us."[3]

In both senses, "the whole" refers to the existence of a people whose force of existence provides the organic conditions of the art form, creating its "motor coordination" as described by Deleuze in the first cinema book. In the absence of the people, whose existence adds the final stroke to the mass artwork that expresses their manner and their perfectibility as a collective (or in moments of crisis, their imperfection and inevitable disintegration, or a retreat into something that resembles fascism), this motor coordination no longer functions, producing a frozen and motionless state, a trance: the actual disintegration of the relation between a people and the political possibilities of the artwork. Given Deleuze's premonition of the decline of the auteur function in modern cinema as a condition for the emergence of a new political cinema, we can find a clear precedent that Deleuze and Guattari located earlier on in Kafka's own treatment of the conditions of literary production in Prague vis-à-vis Weimar Classicism. The question I will ask is whether this characterization of "the political" found in Deleuze and Guattari's earlier invention of the concept of "minor literature" still pertains to the relationship between art and politics today.

In response to this question, let's turn to Deleuze and Guattari's original argument and repeat the three defining characteristics of what is called a minor literature before applying this concept to the current context. Before listing characteristics, it is important to underline the fact that Deleuze and Guattari first subtract the subject of enunciation that pertains to a minor language. As they write, "a minor literature doesn't come from a minor language; it is rather that which a minority constructs within a major language."[4] (This will be important for Kafka's own understanding of the literature of minorities writing in German.) Turning now to the three major characteristics of minor literature:

- The first characteristic of minor literature is a high coefficient of deterritorialization (i.e., form of expression);
- The second characteristic of minor literature is that everything is political (i.e., relation of modality—real, possible, necessary);
- The third characteristic of minor literature is that everything assumes a collective value (i.e., form of communicability, *sensus communis*).

Taking up the second major characteristic, the nature of necessity must be understood according to the category of modality in the Kantian sense of distinguishing between real, possible, and necessary experience. An experience might be possible and yet still not exist; however, what is necessary is the condition that determines all possible and real (or existing) experience. In other words, the axiom employed by Deleuze and Guattari in defining the experience of the political is an expression of the third modality of experience; therefore, *every individual concern is necessarily political*, almost in the sense that the necessary condition of all empirical experience is space and time:

> The individual concern thus becomes all the more necessary, indispensable, magnified, because a whole other story is vibrating within it. In this way, the family triangle connects to other triangles—commercial, economic, bureaucratic, juridical—that determine its values. . . . What in great literature goes on down below, constituting a not indispensable cellar of the structure, here takes place in the full light of day, what is there a matter of passing interest for a few, here absorbs everyone *no less than as a matter of life and death*.[5]

Deleuze and Guattari strategically *exaggerate* the political signification of the individual's concern, as if the content of any personal struggle (especially in the Oedipal family) were imminently political (i.e., "no less than as a matter of life and death") and the real nature of this struggle were immediately apparent to everyone involved (i.e., "in the full light of day"). This claim is only further exaggerated by minority literary critics who have adopted the claim that "the personal is political" as a major axiom of political interpretation.

As Stanley Corngold argues, by telescoping local struggles that move outward from the Oedipal family through social space, to the point where their signification is overdetermined as a life-and-death struggle, Deleuze and Guattari clearly exaggerate the political value that can be attached to individual or familial struggles over identity.[6] Of course, one could immediately respond that this tendency can easily be found in Kafka's stories as well; it can certainly be represented in stories like "The Judgment" and "The Metamorphosis," in which a certain familial struggle inevitably becomes a matter of life or death for the protagonist. For example, Georg leaps to his suicide immediately after hearing the judgment of his father, and Gregor dies from a wound inflicted by his sister. In *The Trial*, Joseph K. wakes one morning to find himself under arrest, and at the end of the day he is *politely* executed; the henchmen carefully fold his shirt before a dagger is plunged into his heart. And yet the question that should concern us is the implicit definition of the "political" as *necessarily* "a matter of life and death." In other words, is this not ultimately a sacrificial (i.e., sovereign) definition of politics, which cannot address the situation of "literary politics" without euphemism or metaphor?

Apart from the fictional representation of the personal struggle in his stories, therefore, we must now ask: what is Kafka's own definition of "literary politics" (the social situation belonging to the literary culture of small nations)? At this point I will turn to the well-known diary entry from December 25, 1911, upon which Deleuze and Guattari base many of their own claims. Kafka writes:

> Since people lack a sense of context, their literary activities are out of context too. They depreciate something in order to be able to look down upon it from above, or they praise it to the skies in order to have a place up there beside it. (Wrong.) Even though something is often thought through calmly, one still does not reach the boundary where it connects up with similar things, one reaches this boundary soonest with politics, indeed, one even strives to see it before it is there, and

often sees this limiting boundary everywhere. The narrowness of the field, the concern too for simplicity and uniformity, and, finally, the consideration that the inner independence of the literature makes the external connection with politics harmless, result in the dissemination of literature within a country *on the basis of political slogans [sich an den politischen Schlagworten festhält]*. There is a universal delight in the treatment of petty themes whose scope is not permitted to exceed the capacity of small enthusiasms and which are sustained by their polemical possibilities. Insults, intended as literature, roll back and forth, [and] among the more violent temperaments they fly back and forth. What in great literature goes on down below, constituting a not indispensable cellar of the structure, here takes place in the full light of day, what is there a matter of passing interest for a few, here absorbs everyone no less than as a matter of life and death.[7]

In this passage, Kafka provides us with at least four definitions of "minority politics," which I will work through backwards in comparison with Deleuze and Guattari's version quoted above.

- First, indeed, there is the statement of an issue that is "a matter of life and death," but the clear reference concerns what Kafka describes as the "liveliness of polemics" that determine the scenes of recognition and judgment in the community of minor literary forms (such as personal conflicts and competition between schools and small magazines).

- The second definition of politics refers to the dissemination of literature by means of "political slogans," which is caused by the "narrowness of the field," the "simplicity and uniformity" of utterances, especially since any external connection with actual politics is ineffectual, "harmless," if not altogether absent due to the lack of national identity.

- Third, it is this condition of the absence of an effective political value attached to literature that directly results in the third definition of "politics": a tendency to locate the external boundary of politics everywhere and even to see it before it is actually there (thus, the most private or personal conflict immediately becomes political, defined as a matter of life and death).
- Finally, the fourth definition refers to the prejudiced character of subjective judgment itself, which seems to saturate and overdetermine every public expression of literary taste or value: the prejudice of depreciating a literary work in order to place oneself above it (to look down on it as a critic) or to praise it in order to place oneself beside it as an equal and thus on the same level as the creator (to bestow upon oneself the very symbolic power of recognition that is the basis of all subjective judgment).

Accordingly, we might view Deleuze and Guattari's claim that in a minor literature everything is necessarily political as a symptomatic reading of Kafka's own descriptions of literary culture of "small nations," but especially with regard to the tendency to exaggerate the external boundary of the political so that it is found to be everywhere, in the same manner that they describe the Oedipal family as a triangle that connects to every other triangle throughout social space until a point of saturation is reached where every private or individual concern is filled with political significance. Here, I simply defer again to Corngold's astute criticisms of Deleuze and Guattari's famous appropriation of this passage to claim that in a minor literature everything becomes a political concern: "In wanting to celebrate this aspect of minor literature—its ineluctably, instantaneously political character—Deleuze and Guattari are required to leave out these last sentences, for they would damage their *valorization* of minor literature on radical grounds. These sentences say that *the literature of small nations disseminates itself often by means of clinging to political slogans*."[8] As I will discuss in chapter 4, it is more than a little ironic that Deleuze and Guattari's own concept of minor literature has been disseminated more or less as a "political slogan" in determining the goals of political interpretation for the past fifty years. Therefore, aside from the symptomatic manner in which Deleuze and Guattari deploy Kafka's own descriptions in their creation of the concept of minor literature—for purely "strategic" reasons, which I will explain later on—their most critical omission is the specific social situation of literary culture that Kafka is depicting.

In the diaries, Kafka's reflections are primarily directed at the literary scene in Prague in which the young and yet unknown Kafka himself took part: Café Savoy, the Jewish Town Hall (where he gave the lecture on Yiddish), and the Hotel Erzherzog Stefan (where he first read "The Judgment" for the newly founded Johann Gottfried Herder Association for the Promotion of Theoretical Interests).[9] This local literary scene would also include the small presses and local journals in which Kafka published, before Max Brod brought him to the attention of Kurt Wolff. Therefore, it is only according to a more realist depiction of these minor institutions of a small literary culture (local conflicts, regional schools, small magazines and independent presses) that one might actually be able to claim, as Deleuze and Guattari do, *that the situation of a minor literature can be characterized as a kind of collective enunciation of free and indirect discourse* (or, according to Jacques Rancière's more recent description of the same phenomenon, the quasi-democratic equality of dissensus in the aesthetic sphere).

As anyone who has actually taken part in these minor spaces of literary production will tell you, they are replete with local and small authorities, anonymous creators, and various nobodies, all of whom aspire to become part of the local literary scene—most often by imitating the style of a major literature, or "writing like X or Y." In fact, in such minor settings it is often difficult, if not impossible, to discern who is a major talent and who is merely an amateur enthusiast, given that the criteria for discerning the quality of literary products have been established by a major literature and its authors. And yet it is precisely because of this state of equality that covers every work produced there and determines its value—or lack thereof—that one might also say that the division between personal or private, on one side, and public or political, on the other, is canceled out. In other words, the personal desire for recognition becomes a collective concern only in the sense that every individual or petty polemic is immediately invested with a highly politicized or potentially collective judgment of value, especially concerning the authenticity and value of the literary expression itself, so that every collective judgment of the work of this or that individual writer actually appears *as if it were a matter of life or death.*

Concerning the actual conditions of minor literature, therefore, we discover that the "liveliness of polemics" is inextricably linked to the personal identity of the writer, a concern of recognition and fame, even at the local level of the neighborhood café, small literary magazine, or school. Moreover, it is just as likely that "political slogans" are employed as a vehicle of this desire for collective recognition. Of course, this does not disqualify this expression of the political from having a truly collective sense of enunciation—*unless one actually believes that the political should be completely divorced from motives of self-interest, or the "private sphere of the individual" replete with all of the petty motives and selfish cares.* Moreover, is this not another way of understanding the statement that the personal becomes a political concern, or that the boundaries between private and political enunciation are erased in the "cramped spaces" where minor literature actually emerges, such that every personal affair is invested with a collective value? According to Deleuze and Guattari's account, as well as the tradition of political interpretation that follows from their understanding of the "bachelor machine," we often find a concerted denial of the reality of the selfish, petty, and highly personal interests that saturate the concrete social fields of literary and political enunciation, creating an unrealistic representation of the conditions for the combination of personal and collective desire in the forms of literature and art. As a result, what is determined as political enunciation in literature is abstracted from all individual content and self-interest, and in place of the individual's personal concern for recognition we are provided an abstract and purely impersonal image of politics.

2

The Principle of "Anti-interpretation"

Before continuing my discussion of the three characteristic of minor literature, I will open a parenthesis and make some direct remarks on Deleuze and Guattari's principle of "anti-interpretation," which has been the subject of much confusion and controversy. Basically, if they define their approach to Kafka as "anti-interpretation," this is because they don't presume that writing is a "text" (a formed substance of expression). Instead, for Deleuze and Guattari, writing is a machine that Kafka is always in the process of constructing, but which also succumbs to periods of breaking down or technical metamorphosis, since, in each case, the writing machine will come up against a limit or deficiency and must be reinvented. Accordingly, there are three parts, or components, found to belong to Kafka's writing machine (the letters, the stories, and the novels), and these are fashioned successively, even though it could be said that Deleuze and Guattari's description is more than a little forced throughout. Moreover, there is a lasting irony in their constant claim that there is "no metaphor" anywhere in Kafka, because their own interpretation of Kafka's letters, diaries, stories, and novels as the technical components of a "machine" is nothing less than a forced metaphor.

At the same time, there is something technically accurate in characterizing Kafka's relation to his own writing mechanically and with the following questions: "What are the components of this literary machine, of Kafka's writing, or expression, machine?"[1] First, to define the specific nature of the literary machine, Deleuze and Guattari distinguish between two kinds of technical machines, both of which relate to the invention of language: the first series of technical machines communicates across vast distances by means of a physical locomotion achieved by a motor function (a horse, a train, an automobile), and the second series reintroduces a ghostly element of communication between people (which can be defined as a "simulated or artificial proximity" that does not erase the actual distances between subjects). The letter technically combines both functions, which is why they call it "an indispensable gear," a motor part of the literary machine, which is why Kafka chooses it as a mode of expression. Moreover, one does not write letters to publish them, and certainly Kafka never intended his letters to be published, much less interpreted as a component of his work.

Kafka is first drawn to the letter as a means of expressing his desire, specifically, as a form of intimacy that maintains the distance between two subjects. Of course, he expresses this desire mostly in his letters to women—first to Felice, then Grete, then Milena—which takes on comic proportions in the impossibility of restoring any actual intimacy (sexual or conjugal), usually in the form of what Deleuze and Guattari call a "topographical obstacle" (coming to Vienna, arriving at a certain hour for a sexual interlude, etc.). It is this ghostly element expressed by writing that is constantly addressed in Kafka's epistolary episodes with women. This becomes properly comic in all of its aspects, including the impossibility that writing can ever restore the natural communication between subjects, as it instead exaggerates the pathetic distance of the medium as a compromise formation, which sooner or later becomes a contract of continuing the relationship. Deleuze and Guattari provide the scenario of a truly Kafkaesque love: a man falls for a woman he has seen only once; a thousand letters immediately ensue, sometimes as many as ten a day, all of which express the impossibility of consummating the affair; the man keeps all of the desperate replies close to him in a trunk (or sleeps with all the letters covering his naked body like a blanket); and finally, after an infinite series of postponements and deferrals, a last letter arrives from the country, and the man knocks the mailman down to prevent its delivery.

According to Deleuze and Guattari, however, the technical machine of the letters always breaks down because its motor function is too dependent on the action of the woman, who must act more like an accomplice than as a subject of real desire—that is, she must continue to keep writing to Kafka and, at the same, accept as a stipulated term of the writing contract that only more letters will arrive in place of the actual subject of Kafka. But the ghosts of writing always threaten to materialize, just as infinite and inexhaustible desire is sooner or later replaced by the demand to be embodied in the subject himself. This subjective form of embodiment—at first, sexual or conjugal—ultimately assumes the juridical form of a judgment, as Felice, then Grete, and later Milena will perceive that Kafka is in love with all the ghosts of enunciation rather than with themselves. In her final "rejecting gesture," Milena will write: "You cannot love me, as much as you would like; you are unhappily in love with your love for me, but your love for me is not in love with you."[2]

It is on this point that Deleuze and Guattari are quite accurate in comparing Kafka to Dracula. From the perspective of the women's accusation, he is a vampire who sends his letters out at night like bats to drink the lifeblood of his victims. Kafka emblematizes—as a constant source of his own self-thematization—the situation of the modernist writer's desire to escape the world of others. This is certainly not divorced from the concupiscence and guilt that belongs to Gyge's magical ring, which provides a cloak of invisibility that, in Kafka's case, becomes Dracula's cape. Accordingly, Kafka himself has been accused of betraying almost every obligation, of breaking every promise and oath, and, in short, of being guilty. In some way, this is what Deleuze and Guattari want to free their Kafka from—as if liberating him from the great confinement of his critics, breaking the chains of interpretation, and allowing Kafka's becoming to take him "head over heels and away," to quote Red Peter in Kafka's story "A Report to an Academy."

In fact, there are two senses of confinement in Kafka: actual confinement by others and self-confinement. As Dimitris Vardoulakis argues concerning Kafka's cages, however, "the first way to misconstrue Kafka's cages is to place an inordinate value on encagement," the form of confinement itself, which also addresses the theological and mystical, or infinite confinement of law and guilt that has been the thick atmosphere of so much of Kafka interpretation historically.[3] As we have witnessed, it is not uncommon for Kafka's readers to fetishize the element of confinement as an expression of their own masochistic tendency, since it is so compulsively present in Kafka's fiction and private writings, which can too easily be mobilized toward such a reading of the cage. The most famous example of this is a letter to Felice Bauer in 1913:

> I have often thought that the best mode of life for me would be to sit in the innermost room of a spacious locked cellar with my writing things and a lamp. Food would be brought and always put down far away from my room, outside the cellar's outermost door. The walk to my food, in my dressing gown, through the vaulted cellars, would be my only exercise. I would then return to my table, eat slowly and with deliberation, then start writing again at once. And how I would

write! From what depths I would drag it up! Without effort! For extreme concentration knows no effort. The trouble is that I might not be able to keep it up for long, and at the first failure—which perhaps even in these circumstances could not be avoided—would be bound to end in a grandiose fit of madness. *What do you think, dearest? Don't be reticent with your cellar dweller.*[4]

Perhaps we can read the above letter in a manner that does not resolve it by transfiguring the author into a monastic priest of high modernist literature who confesses both a warning to his mistress and a sense of consolation mixed with humor. The self-description of the "cellar dweller" is Kafka's way of communicating to Felice his unconscious need to write. He is telling her that in order to be with him, she would have to accept—to at least accommodate, if not to become a willing accomplice and conspirator for—this innate need on the level of his animality. Thus, the figure of the cellar dweller forges a kind of hostage-taking relation with Felice, which she will eventually reject in order to escape Kafka's own enforced confinement.

Nevertheless, to highlight the scene of moral judgment or accusation fails to grasp the erotic phenomenology of the letters themselves, which constantly introduce the features of animality and comic laughter, since the separation of the subject of enunciation and the subject of the statement that is technically performed functions precisely to ward off or elide what Emmanuel Levinas calls "the face" (i.e., ethical signification). As Levinas writes in *Totality and Infinity*, "the face fades, and its impersonal and inexpressible neutrality is prolonged, in ambiguity, into animality. The relations with the Other are enacted in play; one plays with the Other as with a young animal."[5] Thus the social meaning of human sexuality is dissimulated by innuendo as he asks Milena, "*I wonder what you're doing now, Monday, at 11 in the evening?*"—just as the furtive appearance of the feminine is returned to an earlier stage of subjectivity without responsibility (as Levinas describes its figure, "this coquettish head, this youth, this pure life 'a bit silly'") when the beloved "quits her status as a person."[6]

In some ways contrary to Deleuze and Guattari's argument, therefore, we can find a dimension of what they call "becoming-animal" already operating in the letters, since Kafka often emphasizes his animality as his attempt to escape the anthropomorphism of sexual difference—as if to constantly remind his victims that he can be no more guilty than the spider who builds a web to trap his prey or the animal who builds the intricate tunnel work of a burrow to confuse and eventually escape its predators. First accepting and playfully entering into the process of metamorphosis enacted by the play of enunciation, in which the subjects exchange places like the musical dogs in the story "Investigations of a Dog," eventually the ethical signification is restored, the function of which is precisely to make the subject of enunciation "responsible for" the subject of the statement, that is, to bind it into an accusative form of identity. Even Dracula's cape cannot shield Kafka from the light streaming from "the face," causing his victims to suddenly startle and awaken to the feelings of shame and humiliation, finally threatening to turn the infinite duration of desire borne by writing into the sordid affair of "your ugly little letters" (Felice).

Of course, Kafka is well aware of his guilt in this whole letter affair, and his first completed story, "The Judgment," is actually a premonition of the impending indictment, as the father accuses the son of inventing, by means of letters, an imaginary friend who lost himself in Russia, but then turns the tables by declaring his devotion to the fictitious son and condemning his real son to death. This judgment receives its most prophetic expression in *The Trial*, concerning the inevitable and impending breaking off of his engagement with Felice and the indefinite sentence of guilt that will follow. And yet the failure of the technical machine of the letters is not as much the final judgment of guilt, which only appears as an inevitable terminus to the affair, but in fact only comprises an interruption, as one subject of enunciation is eventually replaced by another, just as Felice is later replaced by Milena, and the letter machine continues to function as it did before but is even more accelerated.

Yet the real problem, which is immanent to the cause of writing itself, is its complete and utter dependency on the letter's arrival and the inevitable breakdowns that will occur when, for whatever reason, the letters stop coming. This is illustrated in two diary entries that occur in December 1913:

> December 19: Letter from F. Beautiful morning, warmth in my blood.

> December 20: No letter.[7]

Two years later, triggered by the breakup with Felice (but also by the war and the general hopelessness and misery that it caused the occupants of Prague, including the shortage of coal, which will be a constant feature of the stories collected in *A Country Doctor*), there is a long period of literary unproductivity that lasts until the winter of 1917. In the fall of that year, we find three decisive entries concerning the final breakdown of the "writing machine" and the need to find another means of locomotion. For example, on September 18 there is one entry: "Tear everything up."[8] The next day, after sending a telegram to Felice, Kafka writes another "letter of farewell," but it is not clear that he mails it because the post office is closed. In the entry of September 19 he compares the letter and the telegram as vehicles of communication: "The frail, uncertain, ineffectual being—a telegram knocks it over, a letter sets it on its feet, reanimates it, the silence that follows the letter plunges it into a stupor."[9] On September 22 there is one entry: "Nothing."[10] Finally, on November 6, four days before the diaries go silent for nearly two years, until the summer of 1919, Kafka writes, "Sheer impotence."[11]

According to Deleuze and Guattari, the technical machine of the letters ultimately fails to realize an "autonomous form of expression" because the letters are too dependent on an external subject of enunciation as their motor. This creates too many breakdowns, too many interruptions, and the forms of the diary and the aphorism are not enough to sustain the writing process (or "machine"). It is around this point that their interpretation of "becoming-animal" offers a temporary stopgap or solution, even though this will ultimately fail as well. Implicitly, Deleuze and Guattari's "interpretation" of the particular writing machine invented by the stories is uncharacteristically direct and is even attached to a simple psychological motive: to exorcise the demon of moral responsibility that fatally condemns the medium itself, that is, to assuage or prevent the implicit guilt and the accusation of vampirism of the letters that inevitably results from the discovery of their secret motive, to avoid the familial or social judgment that constantly lurks outside the burrow like a predator, the presence of which, on a purely practical level, causes an interruption of the writing process. (And perhaps it is only this last obstacle that concerns Kafka the most.) For this reason, another motor function must be invented to replace the subject of enunciation of the letters—one that is more reliable, not dependent on external desire, and not prone to intervals when the letters do not come and to the intense state of suffering and desperation that this creates, as demonstrated in the often comic and hysterical complaints on those days when no letter or telegram (in the case of Milena) arrives.

But how and in what sense can we understand that the animal, or "becoming-animal," provides Kafka with what they call an "autonomous motor"? In order to respond to this question, let's recall once more the two technical machines of communication with which we began: first, the physical communication that restores proximity between two subjects by means of locomotion (a horse, a carriage, a train), and second, the ghostly supplement of written communication (the letter, the telegram). However, it is obvious that the second technical form is still too dependent upon the first to deliver the message. On top of this, there is a third technical form that is especially important for Kafka's special use of the enunciation of the letters as a motor function for his own writing machine. In other words, we must imagine the arrival of the letter or telegram to become a vehicle of expression that Kafka will employ to send his own message by return trip; the letters themselves become a kind of technical machine of the first order, and Kafka will mount the original enunciation of each letter, substituting his own "I" for the original subject of the statement, even quoting sentences or phrases like carriers, then slapping its hindquarters as he sends the letter back to its owner with his own "I" as a new rider. Even when the letters are interrupted, the diaries furnish the writing machine with new statements, and the stories will begin often by Kafka mounting fragments from the diaries and then off we go!

The letter, the diary, the notebook—these are the vehicles of expression that provide an image of movement to the act of enunciation, which, in the form of the story, transports the "I" from point A to point B and, in the narrative, from "this happened" to "then this happened" and so on. It is important to observe, however, that the same situation of being too dependent upon an external subject of enunciation in the case of the letters is constantly referred to as the same situation in the diaries concerning the impossibility of writing, as if all writing were completely dependent on an external cause or on another subject. Thus, in the diaries we have just as many entries that report "no letter" as we have entries that simply state "nothing." But let me be clear: I am simply observing that the letter-writing machine is highly productive, as volumes of Kafka's letters can attest, and that even the slightest interruption will only produce more letters, as when a letter does not arrive on a particular day, and Kafka sends five letters in hysterical complaint. As an example, I quote the letter to Felice from March 25, 1914:

> Dearest F., in your last letter (how long have I sat motionless over that word, wishing you were here!) there is a sentence that is fairly clear to me from every angle; this hasn't happened for a long time. It concerns the apprehensions you feel about sharing life with me. You don't think—or perhaps you merely wonder whether, or perhaps you merely want to hear my views about it—that in me you will find the vital support you undoubtedly need. There is nothing straightforward I can say to that. I may also be too tired just now (I had to wait for your telegram until 5 P.M. Why? What's more, contrary to your promise, I had to wait as long as 24 hours for your letter. Why?) and far beneath my tiredness too happy about your letter.[12]

The situation of writing is different for the stories and the novels, which almost seem completely dependent on an external cause, as if thoughts only arrived as dreams or messages sent from a dead letter writer. I refer to the famous diary entry from December 6, 1922, which attests to writing's complete "lack of independence of the world," that is, "its dependence on the maid who tends the fire, on the cat warming itself by the stove; it is even dependent on the poor old human being warming himself by the stove. All these independent activities ruled by their own laws; only writing is helpless, cannot live in itself, is a joke and a despair."[13]

I now return to our earlier problem: what happens when this technical means of enunciation—the letter machine—grinds to a halt, and the diaries break off. This occurs in the fall of 1916 and continues for almost a full year, until July. And yet something occurs in the intervening winter, which marks what is likely Kafka's most productive period of writing—when he moves to the small apartment on Alchemists Lane and writes with frost biting his fingers due to the lack of coal, even burning drafts of the manuscripts of *A Country Doctor* for heat. Let me turn to the story that best represents Kafka's discovery of a new vehicle of expression, "A Country Doctor." Immediately we notice something that might refer directly to the status of the technical machine we have been discussing: *a dead horse*. "Wrapped up in furs with the bag of instruments in my hand, I was already standing in the courtyard ready for the journey; but the horse was missing—the horse. My own horse had died the previous night."[14]

Almost just as immediately—and everything happens in this narrative either instantly or following an incredibly slow duration, or both at once—a pair of new horses emerges from an abandoned pigsty in the courtyard, followed by a groom who is running out on all fours like a dog, and who will play a critical role in the narrator's thoughts. Then, a comical bit of slapstick immediately ensues in the act of hooking up these "unearthly horses" to their "earthly carriage." The groom attacks the servant girl and leaves a row of red teeth marks on her cheek. The doctor threatens the groom with the whip but stays his hand, realizing that he is only a stranger coming to his aid. "Climb in!" says the groom, once the horses are harnessed. "I'll take the reins," replies the doctor. "Right, I'm staying," retorts the groom, clapping the horses on their hindquarters and then immediately giving chase to poor Rosa, who has already run screaming into the house with "an accurate premonition" of what's going to happen next, and is now running through the corridors putting out all the lights "to make herself impossible to find."[15]

Yet in the midst of all this commotion, a thought has occurred to everyone in attendance, including the doctor himself and the servant girl, but we must also include the reader: "Where on earth did these horses come from, and are they horses at all?" This is especially in question because they emerge miraculously from an abandoned pigsty, which is too low for horses to occupy, and are described as having the long necks and non-equine heads of camels. The narrative provides two answers to the question of these unearthly creatures. Later in the story, the narrator speculates that they were sent to the doctor by the gods to assist him in his critical journey, and for good measure, the gods provided not just one but two horses, along with the gift of a groom, who turns out to be more of a nuisance than a help. (As we know from Kafka's other fables, such are the gifts of the gods: a mixture of necessity and childishness.) However, the most practical explanation comes from the mouth of the servant girl, who says to the doctor in an example of free indirect discourse, "One doesn't know the sorts of things one has stored in one's own house."[16] In the following, I will link this statement to the technical discoveries that are evidenced in the story.

On the first and most evident level, as many critics have already commented, the new vehicle of expression and the formal discovery of "A Country Doctor" is the first-person narration. Certainly, the "I" of the narrator is one of those things that have been left in the pigsty referred to by the servant girl. The first statement, "I was in great difficulty," followed by the description of a "becoming more immobile," could be employed as a generic situation that one can find in the earlier stories, though described from a third-person narrator. For example,

Kafka uses the first-person perspective to recapitulate the same difficult situation of immobility in "The Metamorphosis": "Gregor Samsa awoke from fitful dreams," and the two rooms of the Samsa family home become the external courtyard and the interior room of "A Country Doctor." Likewise, in the opening of *The Trial* we are also presented in the third-person narrative with the figure of Josef K., who is awakened to find himself in a situation of "great difficulty": "Someone must have been telling lies about Josef K., for without having done anything wrong, he was arrested one fine morning."[17] In other words, it is the generic event "of a great difficulty," as the narrator says, which I have described above in reference to the technical machine of the letters and the diaries, that is, the feared and anxiety-producing situation that occurs when a letter does not arrive, and the promise of an even more foreboding and life-threatening situation that this state will become permanent—in other words, when the words will no longer come, which spells the end of writing. Kafka has discovered a remarkable means of constructing what Deleuze and Guattari call an "autonomous writing machine," that is, of sending a message to himself without the need to depend on any technical machine of the first order—neither an external means of communication, nor an independent subject of enunciation, nor another "I." Thus, we will also find different versions of this image repeated: the gesture of the doctor whispering in the ear of the young patient in "A Country Doctor," the doorkeeper bending down to deliver the final message in the ear of the man from the country in "Before the Law," and, in "Message from the Emperor," the description of a message (or a letter) sent from a dying emperor and the impossibility of its arrival from the center of the earth, given the throngs of people crammed into each inner courtyard. "And yet," this fable ends, this time in the second person, "you sit in a window one evening and dream the message to yourself."[18]

Second, we come to the horses themselves, or to Kafka's animals generally, as present in the other stories written during this period and collected in *A Country Doctor* (1919). In the story Kafka chooses to lead the volume, which seems to have been intended to pair up with "A Country Doctor"—the two stories are published together that year in the journal *Marsyas*—we are immediately presented with the figure of a riderless horse: Bucephalus, the charger of Alexander the Great. His unearthly origin has also been the subject of much speculation, but of note is that he was described as having the head of an ox, perhaps bearing an allusion to the horses with the heads of camels described in the next story. The horse, the camel, or, more generically, the genre of the animal fable as a favored vehicle of expression is not as much invented by Kafka as found lying around the house or in the cellar, or, more accurately, in the barn or pigsty. However, Kafka's transformation of this genre of the animal fable uniquely represents a new kind of technical machine that exhibits an instantaneous image of movement between points A and B, or rather, substitutes an external movement that restores the proximity between two subjects with an internal and instantaneous apprehension of proximity. In short, it represents Kafka's adaptation of "metamorphosis" or "transformation" (*Verwandlung*), that is, the mechanism of the classical animal fable à la Greque, which Kafka employs as distinctive movement-image; it folds exterior distance and interior, or subjective, proximity while leaving them separate and apart. Thus, we have the image of the journey between the doctor's courtyard and the farmyard of the patient in the next village: "I am already there, as if the farmyard of my invalid opens up immediately in front of my courtyard gate."[19]

Third, in Kafka's more private symbolism, the animals simply represent the stories and fables themselves as distinctive creatures. In many conversations and in the letters to Max

Brod, Kafka's supreme image of the vehicle of expression in the completed stories is a row of circus horses, each of which has its front hooves on the rump of the preceding one, walking on their hind legs to the amazement of the audience (an image that is repeated later in the series of the musical dogs). This characterization is also used in the story "Eleven Sons," each son referring to a different story in the collection and each with his own personality and unique characteristics. Therefore, each story is an animal (e.g., horse, camel, dog, beetle, mole, ape, etc.); these animals belong to Kafka's family, just as each story expresses the unique characteristics of a father's own sons, and we should recall the menacing characteristics of the last son, who is to destroy the family by replacing the father. But here I pull back on the reins and stop myself abruptly with this last claim. Is this allegory? Is this metaphor? In other words, does the horse allegorically represent a new component of expression that now belongs to the writing machine? Do the horses represent metaphorically a new vehicle of expression and, minimally, the technical and narrative form of the stories written during this period? Of course my answer would be yes, contrary to everything that Deleuze and Guattari claim, and even though, as I have argued, their own interpretation of this discovery simply comes down to another allegory of writing: that of "becoming-animal." And yet, even if we have acknowledged the allegorical or metaphoric function of the animals in these stories, this still does not exhaust their significance or their meanings from one instance to the next, since one of the most remarkable things about Kafka's use of these symbols is their protean and constantly changing sense. This includes his use of private symbolism, elements from the previous stories (such as the fur coat from the picture in Gregor's room, which becomes the doctor's coat; the horses that become camels; or the dogs that become jackals and then again musical dogs), and even citations of statements from the letters themselves, combined in a manner that strongly resembles the syntactic construction of dream work.

Fourth, it has been well noted by critics that the main distinction of the stories written in 1917 is the absence of any explicit allusion or even allegorical representation of Kafka's personal drama with his father, the family, or the conjugal relationship with Felice Bauer that supposedly comprises the psychological content of "The Judgment," "The Metamorphosis," and the drafts of *The Trial* written in 1914. But is this entirely true? On the contrary, as already outlined, I would say that one situation of great difficulty is simply exchanged for more generic and multiple situations that all have to do with the problem of immobility (a dead horse or the death of the rider, a difficult or impossible journey, an ancient enmity, a message from a dead emperor or gaining admittance to the inner court of the law, the cares of a family man or father, a fratricide, the dream of the murder of Joseph K., a cage with no way out). But is the entire question of desire and paranoid jealousy that often motivates the frantic letters to Felice completely exorcised by the discovery of a form of expression that seems no longer dependent on an external will that would need to be subjugated and tamed by a rider? Of course, this last allusion evokes the depictions of Alexander taming Bucephalus as well as Plato's allegory of the charioteer, both of which Kafka employs as one of the things that one might find in a pigsty—except that in his comic rendition of the latter, the black horse has become unbridled and no longer harnessed to the chariot at all, but is metamorphosed into the wild and vulgar groom back at home mounting the poor servant girl. His head is still tortured by the thoughts of the unbridled groom ravaging Rosa, and the image of the unearthly horses pulling an earthly carriage is, in the end, replaced by a row of horses riding single file, with the narrator in front riding naked with the carriage dragging his fur coat behind him in the snow. Likewise, there is an ironic admission typical of all of Kafka's endings—an extreme pessimism that this new discovery will not exactly be a complete liberation from the old fears, since the new vehicle of expression no longer goes directly from point A to point B but only manages to go in circles, ever widening and eventually encompassing the entire city of Prague, as in the opening of *The Castle*.

Fifth, and finally, at this point we must turn to directly address the figure of the young servant girl, Rosa, who properly assumes the function of a signifier, given, as many critics have observed, that it is also the color of the vagina-shaped wound, "the size of the palm of one's hand opened," "as if cut in a tight corner with an ax," that suddenly appears on the right side of the "region of the hip" of the young invalid: "Rose colored, in many different shadings, dark in the depths, brighter on the edges, with uneven patches of blood, open to the light like a mining pit." In fact, if this were a psychoanalytic interpretation we would spend a great deal of time discussing the significance of placing this flower on the right side of the region of the hip, which could refer to sexual difference, which is further reinforced in the description of the naked doctor lying against the wall near the patient on the same side as the wound. However, one does not need to be a psychoanalyst to see this association, which appears in the same manner as an obsessional compulsive idea that torments the mind of the doctor: "Rosa!" However, one does not know if the name refers to the servant girl or to the actual wound itself. In fact, this idea is given a further hallucinatory effect in that it suddenly and somewhat mysteriously materializes as an effect of illumination from the upper regions, like a vision from the gods sent through the medium of the horses whinnying in the moonlit window. It is this hallucinatory status that begs the following questions: Is it the obsessional idea of Rosa, the servant girl being molested at home by the disgusting groom, that materializes into the rose-colored wound on the hip of the young patient? Or rather, is it the wound itself that the doctor fails to see at first, being distracted in his duty by the obsessive thought that suddenly reminds him of Rosa? Any answer leads to an interminable equivocation, or to a game of fort-da, if you like, concerning the meaning of the signifier Rosa. The wound is here, while Rosa is there. The doctor's thoughts are there with Rosa, while his duty to heal the young patient's interminable wound is here.

Nevertheless, if the wound is made to refer to the embodiment of sexual difference, the cause of desire, then the statement of the young patient is given further irony: "I came into the world with a beautiful wound; that was all I was furnished with."[20] Finally, if we refer back to the description of the wound close up, where we find "worms, as thick as my little finger, themselves rose colored and spattered with blood," might we not find the most grotesque but literal representation of male sexual hysteria in the vision of Rosa—the girl, the wound—that torments the doctor throughout the story?[21] Could this hallucinatory and obsessional idea not also evoke the thoughts concerning Felice that must have tormented Kafka during this period, between the first and second engagements, a period when Felice was unharnessed from the letter machine that demanded that all of her desire be focused on the subject of Kafka himself? Thus, her own vaginal wound would be opened to the row of unwelcome suitors and disgusting want-to-be-grooms who, as our doctor claims, might come after me but "can never replace me" (a statement, by the way, quoted directly from one of the letters). Perhaps, perhaps. Regardless, given the context for our interpretation, it may be important to observe that Deleuze and Guattari never mention this last association, despite their attention to the letters, and certainly never make any reference to this rose-colored wound, even though this same "unmentionable wound" reappears in the last story of the collection, "A Report to an Academy," as a wound on the region of the groin of Red Peter that becomes a source of shame, embarrassment, and in short, the ape's "Humanity!" Regardless, as we know from Deleuze and Guattari's subsequent writings concerning sexuality and its multiple and symbolic symbols that they would rather see a field of vaginas than one singular wound, or "splinter in the flesh."

I will now close my parenthesis by outlining three major criticisms of Deleuze and Guattari's interpretation of Kafka. Did I say "interpretation"? Yes, I did. Despite all the claims to the contrary, what they offer at this point is clearly an interpretation of what they call Kafka's "animalistic stories." Moreover, despite all their protests against psychoanalytic, allegorical, or symbolic interpretation—but especially the often hysterical and manic defense against psychoanalysis and what they call "Oedipal interpretation"—there are clearly metaphors and symbols operating in Kafka's stories. Accordingly, in response to their assertion that "Kafka deliberately kills all metaphor, all symbolism, all signification, no less than all designation," one can interpret this statement following the same principle of Freudian analysis concerning the species of "negation": that it expresses a repressed content in consciousness under the condition that it is accompanied by a strong negation (which, by the way, Freud also finds in the structure of jokes and their relation to the unconscious).[22] Therefore, when Deleuze and Guattari say "there are absolutely no metaphors, no allegory!" we should substitute the statement "Absolutely, there are metaphors, there are allegories and symbols." But here the question becomes the specific nature of symbolic or metaphorical substitutions that Kafka invents in the stories as well as their genetic and literary (or mythical) composition and inheritance, especially in his symbolic use of animals. Of course, one cannot interpret what one refuses to see in the first place. This could be called, in a certain sense, a *maxim of interpretation*.

I will now conclude this digression on the principle of anti-interpretation by listing my three primary objections. First, Deleuze and Guattari are themselves far too allegorical in reading the entire psychological drama of the stories as a failed attempt to escape the Oedipal impasses of familial and social identity through the subjective process of the becoming-animal. Thus, their allegorical interpretation of the subjective process engaged by Kafka himself is telescoped on three stories that they use to illustrate both the discovery and the ultimate limitations of the stories, which they reduce to the process of becoming-animal: "The Metamorphosis" (written in December 1913), "A Report to an Academy" (the last story in *A Country Doctor*, written in 1917), and "The Burrow" (written in 1922). However, it is the story from the middle period from which they derive the overall formula of the becoming-animal as "a way out," "a line of escape, and not freedom," according to Red Peter, which is taken to represent in a patently allegorical manner an escape from the impasse of Oedipal subjectivity. Nevertheless, they also claim that the stories ultimately fail in achieving this desire by either closing in on themselves too perfectly (as exemplified in "A Country Doctor") or in opening out to an indefinite and infinite multiplicity (as exemplified perhaps in the aphoristic stories such as "Message from the Emperor"), even though, as they say, this will lead directly to "the machinic assemblages that are no longer animal and can only be given proper treatment in the novels."[23]

Second, I would say that Deleuze and Guattari's treatment of the stories as an "intermediary vehicle" in the transition from the letters to the novels (the genre they privilege, of course) is not only inaccurate for being too telescoped on the so-called Oedipal drama of subjectivity but is also far too teleological. As any biographer of Kafka and his writings will tell you, the phases of the letters, the stories, and the so-called novels (*Amerika*, *The Trial*, and *The Castle*)—but also the diaries, the notebooks, and the aphorisms—overlap so much that one cannot say that there was a unidirectional process (nor what Deleuze and Guattari call a "life plan" corresponding to the development of the writing process à la Kleist). As we know, large portions of *The Trial* were drafted during the period of the letters to Felice and before the stories collected in *A Country Doctor*, and the letters themselves resume later to Grete and especially with Milena. In fact, it is interesting to see how Deleuze and Guattari go to great pains to criticize the edition of *The Trial* under the hands of Brod (who is also blamed for many of the earlier theological interpretations of Kafka's works), particularly for the inclusion of the ending from an earlier dream fragment that appears in the diaries. But much of their criticism can also be understood to apply to its failure to correspond with their interpretation of the novelistic genre as successfully breaking through the impasses of the letters and the animal stories (since the execution or murder of Joseph K. too much resembles the tragic death of Gregor Samsa).

Third, in response to the argument that all the stories are animalistic, even though there are not animals in all the stories, or that "the animal is the object par excellence of the story," I have always found this claim to be a bit exaggerated and bombastic, which, in many ways, is just as exaggerated or clumsy as psychoanalytic interpretation. Certainly, beginning with "The Metamorphosis," but especially in the stories collected in *A Country Doctor*, animals and a certain inheritance of the animalistic fable play a key role in Kafka's adaptation and transformation of the story genre. But to reduce all the instances to one process of subjectivity (of Kafka, the writer, or the content of the stories themselves) is clearly an exaggeration, although, as I have already suggested above, perhaps this was Deleuze and Guattari's strategy as well!

3

The Tautology of Literary History

Now that we have a better understanding of the function of the components of expression in Deleuze and Guattari's overall interpretation, let us return to the first characteristic in Kafka's own definition of the literary culture of small nations (i.e., minority peoples), which is that it is both "incomplete" and "seemingly broad in scope." As Kafka immediately qualifies, this is because it lacks the influence of "outstanding talents."[1] For example, Yiddish literature in Warsaw is an instance of a literature without major talents according to Kafka, one exemplarily not dominated by a single major talent, the struggle with which might conceivably define its whole future direction. In other words, Yiddish literature does not have its Goethe; therefore, it does not live in the shadow of a single indomitable father figure.[2] As a result of this lack of a dominant paternal function, minor literature has the simple appearance of being unusually "broad in scope," which can also be described as a kind of free indirect agency of collective enunciation; however, this is primarily because its authors are, for the most part, anonymous, unknown, even "mediocre and amateurish" (the last description is Kafka's, not mine).

On the other hand, comparing this situation of Czech literature in Prague or Yiddish literature in Warsaw (which are the primary subjects of the diary entries of 1911), German literature may actually be handicapped by its own major writers—and, according to Kafka, especially by the paternal figure of Goethe. As Kafka writes:

> Goethe probably retards the development of the German language by the force of his writing. Even though prose style has often traveled away from him in the interim, still, in the end, as at present, it returns to him with strengthened yearning and even adopts obsolete idioms found in Goethe but otherwise without any particular connection with him, in order to rejoice in the completeness of its unlimited dependence.[3]

Nevertheless, Kafka sees distinctive advantages and disadvantages as a result of the lack of this paternal function in the literature of minorities. The advantages were already noted above: the relative "democracy of talents"—in minor literatures, we should remember, minority writers are not all extraordinarily talented, but this implies that they are not all extraordinarily untalented either!—and thus the relative freedom to develop in any future direction lacking the burden of official literary history. On the other hand, there are distinct disadvantages as well, namely, the risk of being unduly influenced by "literary fashions" and by the introduction of "foreign writers and works," which is less a temptation for writers in a major literature. "This is plain," writes Kafka, "in a literature rich in great talents, such as German . . . where the worst writers limit their imitation to what they find at home."[4] Thus, if there is *seemingly* a more democratic relationship between the writer and the people in a minor literature, it is primarily because both subjects are already defined in a secondary or tertiary position according to the conditions of a major language and its literary history. As Nicholas Thoburn also observes: "This 'cellar' of polemics, intrigues, and everyday concerns substitutes for the grand histories or traditions that occupy national literatures, since without a coherent identity or people, a relation to anything that minorities might describe as *their* history is at most opaque, broken, and uncertain."[5]

In this regard, Fredric Jameson was absolutely correct in his observation that the exemplarity of Kafka (as well as other early modernist writers like Proust, Joyce, and Durrell), is because there was no pre-given model or archetype for connecting the political and social situation of the writer. He writes:

> The first modernists had to operate in a world in which no acknowledged or codified social role existed for them and in which the very form and concept of their own specific "works of art" were lacking. . . . Such imitation was unavailable to the classical modernists, whose works designate their process of production as an analogical level of allegory, in order to make a place for themselves in a world which does not contain their "idea"; this formal auto-referentiality is then utterly different from the poems about poetry and novels about artists in which the late-modernists designate themselves in their content.[6]

In the case of earlier modernists like Proust and Joyce, this singularity accounts for the originality of the writer as a vocation, especially, as opposed to the late modernists like Beckett or Nabokov, whom he seems to discount where the vocation of the writer in self-imposed exile was already a cliché. At the same time, Jameson's claim that Kafka's exceptionalism as a classical modernist writer was the lack of any previous model is certainly not true. As is documented throughout the diaries and the letters to Brod, Kafka's specific problem was the existence of *too many models*, all of which Kafka rejects in favor of constructing what Deleuze and Guattari call the "bachelor machine."

What Jameson opposes most of all is what Deleuze and Guattari famously define as a leading or cutting edge of deterritorialization, as if the bachelor and the writer are beings who always appear on the edge of any family or group, always at the margins of the social bond, and consequently also in direct contact with revolutionary "becoming" and new collective forms of enunciation. Taking up this claim in relation to Kafka's story "Josephine, the Mouse Singer," which Deleuze and Guattari often refer to as an allegory of this process, the Czech-Slovakian critic Michaela Fišerová has written the following:

> On the one hand, Kafka's dog-researcher calls for a common *musical science* that will replace his individual solitary researches; the hymnal singing emphasizes "revolutionary" fight for the united "voice" of the nation, the unified existence in multiplicity. In this sense, also Josephine the singing mouse joins the movement from the animal as individual to the animal pack or collective multiplicity: she gives up on the particularity of her singing in order to disappear in the collective enunciation, the chorus of "countless crowd" of national heroes. But, on the other hand, if we admit that Kafka kept on cultivate his own work as a kind of solitary exceptionality, we can find his conception of the literary plural even more tangled. While the romantic fight for unity and purity of the national language—for the choral unification in multiplicity—was a motor of national revolutions, Kafka intentionally deformed the national language. Kafka keeps his mistrust: his "minority" isn't proposed in the sense of any national or even nationalist dream. In Deleuze's reading, Kafka's minority is composed of voices which inhabit the worlds he alone understands and "carries in his head." Such a singular minority can produce a singular literary style; it doesn't establish new nations, and thus it doesn't enable any positive conception of politics.[7]

Moreover, as result of its most general and mythic signification within the framework of a modernist ideology, the "bachelor machine" has especially distorted the position of the writer in the postcolonial field of literature (the writer as a stranger or foreigner, even in relation to his or her own people or race). In many cases, this has led to predetermination of the position of the minority and postcolonial writer, and of any minority expression for that matter, as having an immanent relation to the politics of the group without any prior determination of its content, a prejudice that sooner or later leads to the discovery of contradictions, either implicit or through the gradual revelation of a number of explicit betrayals. This has led to an entire range of unfortunate "complications" that has surpassed even the intensity of the debates surrounding the French socialist or leftist writer in "Situation of the Writer in 1947," which Sartre was addressing with his conception of a "literature of commitment."

To their credit, Deleuze and Guattari are careful to provide an accurate account of the literary context that determined the various possibilities available to both Kafka and the Jewish writers in Prague and Warsaw at the end of the Habsburg Monarchy. To offer just a few examples, there was the tradition formed by the members of the Prague School (Leppen, Meyrenk, Kisch, Werfel, Brod, Hasvek, and the younger Rilke), but also the German of Goethe and Kleist. There were the emergent Czech popular and nationalist literatures, the Yiddish folk literature, and the popular Yiddish theater of Löwy. Moreover, as is the case of every writer, there is also the presence of other foreign writers who might serve as models or influences and who do not immediately belong to his context and situation in Prague. For example, Kafka admired Dickens and used his work as a model for his first novel, *Amerika*, although Deleuze and Guattari will argue that only Kleist can be regarded as the master who deeply influenced Kafka. They write:

He doesn't want to create a genealogy, even if it is a social one, à la Balzac; he doesn't want to erect an ivory tower, à la Flaubert; he doesn't want "blocks," à la Dickens. . . . The only one he will take as his master is Kleist, and Kleist also detested masters; but Kleist is a different matter even in the deep influence that he had on Kafka. We have to speak differently about this influence.[8]

Following the various descriptions of influences offered in this passage, let us now return to the concrete social space of literary production of a minor literature in order to accurately portray the real conditions of a national (or political) literature that Kafka reflected on in relation to his own situation in Prague, as well as in comparison with the Yiddish literature of Warsaw. First, it is full of mediocre talents and anonymous or highly localized or regional authors, and it is precisely because there is no "outstanding individual genius" who would also serve as a dominating and paternal figure that Kafka finds its compensatory strength in what he calls its "liveliness" (*Lebhaftigkeit*). Moreover, "liveliness" is primarily characterized by its polemical nature as well as by a degree of intense resentment (which is a vital sign of equality between members of the same community), which results from the absence of the paternal figure of genius. In other words, what an anonymous writer craves most is the recognition from all the other writers in attendance, but the social and aesthetic problem specific to minor literature is that it lacks dominant criteria of judgment to produce social recognition. Consequently, no one is empowered to judge (i.e., to establish the symbolic function of identity or recognition that the paternal function provides in a major literature), which then becomes the psychological source of resentment and petty polemics.

Thus we can summarize the above characteristics of "minor literature" (or the literature of "small nations"), which are drawn directly from Kafka's own descriptions rather than those offered by Deleuze and Guattari:

- First, what is called a minor literature is broad in scope because its development lacks a distinctive or defining presence of an outstanding talent. By contrast, a major literature is narrow in scope because its major talents will serve to guide its development, thus "narrowing" its future possibilities;
- Second, what is called a minor literature is "incomplete" (i.e., lacking the major form of a canon or literary history); however, this also means it is relatively free to develop in several different directions in the future, whereas the future of a major literature is relatively closed off by its "unlimited dependence" on its major authors and the major structures that are responsible for creating the dialectic between what T. S. Eliot calls "tradition and the individual talent."

As a contemporary point of comparison, I will take up Jacques Rancière's more recent definition of aesthetic politics: "Politics exists when the figure of a specific subject is constituted, a supernumerary subject in relation to the calculated number of groups, places, and functions in a society. This is summed up in the concept of the *demos*."[9] In the official context of literary history, the "supernumerary subject" is the major author who represents a second "supernumerary subject" (nation, ethnicity, etc.) for a "number of groups, places, and functions in society." (This operation allows one to say, e.g., "Yiddish Literature," "Czech Literature," "Middle–High German Literature," and "Literature of the *Weimarer Klassik*," but also "American Literature," "African American Literature," "Feminist Literature," "Postcolonial Literature," etc.). If we try to apply Rancière's definition of politics in the context of literary production as Kafka describes its specific form of *dissensus* (including petty polemics, personal insults, political slogans, etc.), we inevitably encounter a problem of objectivity, since the real social character of literary production has disappeared in favor of the authors and works that survived as monuments of literary history. Rancière locates this disappearance alongside the shift of perspective from "forms of making" to "modes of sensibility" at the end of the eighteenth century (e.g., as this shift is already defined in Dufrenne's *The Phenomenology of Aesthetic Experience*). As he observes, "this paradox of the politics of art refers back to the very paradox of its definition in the aesthetic regime of art, in which the 'things' called art are no longer defined, as before, by the rules of a practice."[10]

The French critic Maryvonne Saison has also addressed this transformation of the objectivity of the artwork. As she writes, "the 'real community' of the public is entirely subordinated to the 'eminent objectivity of the art work': works of art have a precedence over the experience they call forth. It's for this reason that . . . he [Dufrenne] concludes: 'the objectivity of the work and the demands it implies [is what] imposes and guarantees the reality of the social bond.'"[11] It is this shift of objective conditions of the artwork and the accompanying disappearance of the practical conditions of aesthetic sociability (*sensus communis aestheticus*) that will set the stage for the mourning of communal sensibility: a sensibility originally belonging to the work of art, followed by a period of melancholy and a proactive search for creating the new conditions of aesthetic sensibility in the name of the people (who are now missing), as in the example of Deleuze and Guattari. According to Rancière, the double bind of this melancholic search represents the hidden dynamic of the modern artwork.

> The "resistance of art" thus appears as a double-edged paradox. To maintain the promise of a new people, it must either

suppress itself, or defer indefinitely the coming of this people. The dynamic of art for the last two centuries is perhaps the dynamic generated by this tension between the two poles of art's self-suppression and the indefinite deferral of the people that it calls forth.[12]

To further illustrate this tension, I will quote at length from Saison's interpretation of this idea of the missing people in relation to the *sensus communis*:

> We must now conclude regarding the potential displacement that is effected by this idea of the missing people in relation to the *sensus communis* and to the hope, at the heart of the aesthetic, of instigating a new sociability by means of art. The sociability specific to the aesthetic regime refers to a consensual community: the public which itself is linked to the double figure of a gathering of individuals and the indistinct mass that they constitute. Such a public is marked with the seal of consensuality. With the idea of the people who are missing, by contrast, dissensus and consensus are linked in a tension that is not able to be resolved. Art intervenes as resistance and dissenting energy founded on a visceral refusal of the consensus. However, it is paradoxically animated by the just as visceral affirmation of a necessary foundation played by the role of the public, but which can only be invoked under the name of the people, and moreover in its absence. It is from the angle of minorization that art acquires its political dimension and not through a given engagement that is claimed to be political: art carries with it the absence and the call of a people. The cry "the people are missing" is only heard after mourning the *sensus communis*.[13]

In both of the above descriptions, perhaps we can now locate a third sense of the refrain "the people are missing," one that is not far removed from Deleuze's own sensibility (since it underlines the tension between major and minor forms of consensus)—a tension that Rancière himself merely reduces to the *either/or* between major and minor forms of agreement, or "police consensus" and "political dissensus":

> Politics and police do not refer to such, but instead to two distributions of the sensible, to two ways of framing a sensory space, of seeing or not seeing common objects in it, of hearing or not hearing in it subjects that designate them or reason in their relation.
>
> The police is that distribution of the sensible in which the effectuation of the common of the community is identified with the effectuation of the properties—resemblances and differences—that characterize bodies and their modes of aggregation. It structures perceptual space in terms of places, functions, aptitudes, etc., to the exclusion of any supplement. As far as politics is concerned, it consists—and consists alone—in the set of acts that effectuate a supplementary "property," a property that is biologically and anthropologically unlocatable, unlocatable, the equality of speaking beings.[14]

The process of canonization that constitutes a major literature is marked by a "seal of consensuality" (*sensus communis* in a majoritarian sense) that guarantees its reality and its form of objectivity for a "public." However, the force of the "whole" itself is now completely assigned to the past and to an indistinct or no longer living sociability between the writer and his or her original community. In place of this living sociability there is only a "public" composed of a population and a "numerical count of individuals" (i.e., a "mass"), both living and dead, that the major literature now supposedly guarantees as a legacy of the objective conditions of the social bond to which they are assigned:

> The classical form of political conflict opposes several "peoples" in one: the people inscribed in the existing forms of the law and the constitution; the people embodied in the State; the one ignored by this law or whose right the State does not recognize and the one that makes its claims in the name of another right that is yet to be inscribed in facts. Consensus is the reduction of these various "peoples" into a single people identical with the count of a population and its parts, of the interests of a global community and its parts.[15]

It is for this reason that major literatures are instituted in schools and universities and that their function is primarily pedagogical, disciplinary, and ideological. As Roland Barthes writes, "literature is what is taught, period. Nobody creates literature except those who profess it. Thus, the history of literature is an essentially academic object which in fact exists only because it is taught."[16] Consequently, the value of political interpretation is primarily moral or didactic, since it often reduces the work to information that is used for propaganda, that is, for the creation of a new set of "order-words" (*mots d'ordre*) in a "language," a "theory," a "structure"—in short, an "ideology"—for interpreting major works and writers in the university. In fact, we might hypothesize that the more a major literature locates its creative types in the duration of the past, the more this will lead directly to an institutionalization of literary history, whether in the university or the major publishing houses. For example, political interpretation can only claim it has criteria to judge the creative act in terms of good and bad models already guaranteed by "a seal of consensuality," even when it has no knowledge of the real conditions of aesthetic production, no matter how much ethnographic work is done to recover the original context.

What has survived from the original context of aesthetic production becomes part of the monumental past of the "great work," which now exists like the silence of a battlefield after the battle is over, that is to say, after all the petty polemics between mostly anonymous creators that were moments of the battle itself have vanished into the oblivion of an unknown and forgotten past. Of course, it is this same immemorial battlefield that has become the favored terrain of much political interpretation today; the feminist or minority critic, for example, will conduct an archaeological expedition to the battlefield in order to uncover hidden victims and to erect the new monuments of unknown and anonymous combatants. However, even this work of monumentalization does not illuminate the real conditions of the original *sensus communis aestheticus*, which could be compared to the original social contract between the writer and his or her particular community (or public). In the best case, the minority critic can only recover a deformed image of this original community in the mirror of the present and is more often than not guilty of fictionalizing the relation between the writer and his or her organic community for ideological reasons, as long as they justify the overall goals of political interpretation.

Of course, we must also acknowledge that major authors and works have survived for various reasons, some of which are either highly arbitrary or prejudiced, either owing to the unconscious production of national genius or taking place in "the cellar of structures" erected by literary history. In other words, the criteria of taste that often represent the historical canonization of "great works" and "major figures" are often, if not always, tautological. This problem is only exacerbated by the fact that the literary-historical approach might very well uncover the mundane political realities from which the artwork is born, but the criteria for the selection of one particular author over another in the canon of national literary tradition has already been distorted. In other words, by the time the historian even begins to study the context from which the artwork emerges, his or her only object of study—again, *this* author, rather than *that* one!—already appears as being determined by the transcendental judgment of History itself. As we know from Kafka, the real criteria for the selection of one author over another exist "in the cellar of a structure" that is influenced by the hidden polemics concerning national identity, including the inclusion or exclusion of minorities in the collective memory work of national culture.

Accordingly, my only criticism of Rancière's version of literary history is that it is restricted mostly to the canon of major French authors—Flaubert, Hugo, Proust, and so forth—and does not address the more anonymous and highly contested zones of minor traditions where there is real *dissensus*. To put this another way, the historian actually begins to describe the historical context only after the process of history is finished. This inevitably leads all literary history into an impasse, since the literary historian always remains unconscious as to the structural determination of his or her own object of study at the commencement of the research. In fact, it is this structure itself that is the true object that only appears at the end of the search, epistemologically speaking, but is hidden at the beginning (i.e., when the historical method is critical and not merely tautological, like the major form of literary history itself).

Let's now return to Kafka's own reflections on this issue. In a diary entry from 1911, he writes:

> The force . . . of a literature poor in its component parts proves especially effective when it begins to create a literary history out of the records of its dead writers. These

writers' undeniable influence, past and present, becomes so matter-of-fact that it can take the place of their writings. One speaks of the latter [their writings] and means the former [their influence], indeed, one even reads [their writings] and sees only [their influence]. But since that influence cannot be forgotten, and since the writings themselves do not act independently upon the memory, there is no forgetting and no remembering again. Literary history offers an unchangeable, dependable whole [*einen Block*] that is hardly affected by the taste of the day.[17]

According to Kafka's original description, literary history is a "block" or a monument, a whole that cannot be separated into discrete moments that would constantly succumb to the forces of forgetting; it is unchangeable in the sense that Shakespeare's influence cannot be removed from the history of English literature, or Goethe's from the larger German literature, without destroying the whole. This influence becomes the cause of the restricted development of major literature—that is, its "narrowness"—and the historian reads the dead writers only to see their influence on the present, just as the contemporary writer cannot act independently upon the memory of the nation (or community), since each major work already comprises an entire duration, an *eternity*.

This underlines the first major characteristic of the literature of small nations: its fragmentary nature. However, we must understand this characteristic according to Kafka's original description, which is somewhat different from Deleuze and Guattari's treatment of this nature in their concept of minor literature. For Kafka, these fragments do not comprise a "consistent whole" (*einen Block*) but instead form a patchwork that grows through the accumulation of individual experience or multiple points of view. And yet it is this defect that also becomes a source of its greatest potential: its "seemingly" broad scope, despite its limited idiolect and population, as well as the fragmentary nature of its "collective assemblage of enunciation," is what allows it to develop in several directions at once. As Corngold observes, "what is at stake in the domestic as well as the national sphere is the redemption of *dissonance* that occurs through a continual articulation of a people with respect to its own experience"; however, "the manufacture of literary history in small nations does not follow any model guaranteeing good results, either as history or as textual knowledge, and hence it is not exemplary."[18]

It is precisely this fragmentary nature that becomes significant in Deleuze and Guattari's account of the "revolutionary becoming" of minor literature, even though it does not lead to a totality that one might dream of in the manner that every minor literature would one day have its own Chaucer, or its own Shakespeare, who would represent the original force that combines language and personae into the embodiment of national character. (Although it seems that every minority critic holds out for this as a hope and form of political equality vis-à-vis the major literature in which a minority tradition is situated.) It is in this regard that the case of Kafka is particularly remarkable, because he does not completely belong to German literature, Czech national literature, or Yiddish literature. Rather, Kafka belongs to all three in a patchwork of internal relations and external literary influences; one might even suspect that a fourth category was invented specifically to account for Kafka's particular case—Borges might be another case—in order to assemble all of these patches together into the new postwar genre of "World Literature."

Nevertheless, perhaps this genre also belongs to what Kafka calls a "narrowing of possibilities" and even prefigured the loss of the original cultural contexts for the category of global literature today. As in the case of the creation of literary history on a national or regional level, the creation of a category of world literature (including the genre of what is called "postcolonial literatures") actually narrows the act of creation itself by also locating the greatest number of its major models in the past, which is to say, outside the present where the contemporary writer belongs (either by fate, by fortune, or simply by unhappy accident) to a major language. In the case of established national traditions, the greater a major literature (e.g., British or German), then the greater the power (*potestas*) of creative possibility is assigned to the past, and hence the lesser the power (*potentia*) of creativity is expected in the present moment. This might be one way of explaining why British and German literature do not seem to produce an equivalent number of major authors today—a fact that might not be easily measured in terms of a national readership but only in terms of which contemporary authors are taught in the universities today as "great literature." Would this lead one to suggest that contemporary British and German literature today share the same conditions as are described as the minor literature of Kafka's day, which is to say, a broadening of more common and mediocre talents, if not an "equalization" or "democratization" of contemporary literary history? (Of course, this remains an untested hypothesis.) Returning to the birthplace of minor literature itself, as Michaela Fišerová has observed, after the Czechoslovakian Velvet Revolution, the contemporary situation in Prague changed as well.

> The art made by dissidents was not minor anymore; on the contrary, today it's the art we celebrate and admire as the most pertinent artistic representation of the normalization period in the post-revolutionary era. What happened to the socialist art? One could say the socialist realism reflected an explicit expectation of comprehensibility of art, which was

able to satisfy the traditionalist taste of masses. On the one hand, the evident resemblance between the visual works of socialist realism and the model pictures of propaganda is the reason why it is taken today for a simple kitsch and definitely pushed towards the non-art. On the other hand, along with the transformation of the political system, the art made by ancient dissidents was transformed into the art made by new elites, who appropriated the positions previously occupied by their old adversaries.[19]

4

The Ethical Duty of the Writer and the Critic

Obviously, the situation of "becoming a writer" today is more overdetermined than it was for Flaubert or Proust, since the social meaning is already given in advance as a possible objective solution to the subject's personal and social contradictions, which in some ways also limits this activity's significance because it is already far too "meaningful." In other words, the project of becoming a writer has a social meaning even before it is a project of writing, or before the question of whether the particular work has merit is raised. This is especially the case for a younger generation of minority and postcolonial writers today, where the role of the writer is already invested with a social and political value, which determines the meaning of this activity in advance. However, when the model is already too determining of the specific activity, then the whole meaning of writing is often reduced to becoming a one-dimensional and clichéd matter of representation (e.g., political allegory). The question of a "style" (which Sartre defined as signification within the contemporary framework of ideology) as well as the question concerning the specific circumstances of a text's production (what Kafka himself called "context") are lost in a presupposition that never explains the real reason a subject first chooses to write as a manner of both taking flight from and, at the same time, engaging with his or her particular social situation. This is true whether or not this situation is defined in sexual terms, ethnic terms, or in some other manner yet to be identified by criticism as worthy of being described as "political" today.

In contrast to Jameson's earlier argument concerning the archetypal modernists, therefore, even before we consider the particular social identity, there is already the objective determination of the writer qua writer, which is to say, the objective and historical conditions of literary enunciation determined by literary history (national, linguistic, popular, ethnic, cultural) that the subject cannot ignore entirely without losing precisely the objective determination of being a writer *in the first place*. Even so-called minority writing has its own particular literary history, which also "narrows" its possibilities. For example, Native American writers must always decide whether or not "to write like Native Americans," which also presupposes the act of choosing certain group memories, common experiences, family relationships, habitual addictions, and so on. It is in this sense that the subjective conditions of enunciation are, in part, bound up with the formal and linguistic possibilities that define historically the particular tradition that the writer inherits. Such inheritances are not reducible to individual conditions of experience and memory, for they already belong to what is essentially a quasi-mythical or impersonal form of collective enunciation that might be compared to "a language." By contrast, what Jameson refers to above as "style" refers only to the "idea" that does not belong to the framework of an existing language or to a given world, and thus the means of expressing the idea must be *invented*.

On the other hand, a writer who is already determined by an objective situation of being a subject must invent a number of creative and purely artificial procedures to escape that situation via literature (which I would qualify as a writing process that is not determined in advance in the same way as the given situation itself is). The fact that the "idea" is not completely determined beforehand—that is, it is not determined by the situation in the same way that the living subject is determined—means that there exists some degree of freedom in the process, even though this relative degree of literary freedom may be quite remote from the real situation experienced by the individual subject. Thus, once again, we must come back to the objective determination of the act of writing in the first place, which always precedes the subjective determination of writing itself.

If the meaning of this specific activity of writing has become too abstract, it is because the answers to the questions "What is writing?," "Why write?," and "For whom does one write?" are given in advance by the framework in which most literature is read today. The content, thus, is always already abstracted and immediately subject to criticism for not being specific enough, which is to say that the meaning and value of the work are given before the actual work itself. Here, Sartre is right to point out that it is not the more or less abstract decision to write but instead the decision to write "in a certain manner" that constitutes the primary criterion for discerning the question of style (in Flaubert's case, the style of becoming-woman, which is not simply a matter of "writing like a woman") as one of how the subject of writing constitutes a movement that is both away from and toward the given situation of being "a subject for others."

At this point, to restrict the scope of our investigation to the contemporary situation that determines the concept of "literature" today, we should refer to the creative writing workshop in the university, where the traditional canon of major literature still functions as exemplary, alongside the highly idiosyncratic and personal tastes of a new class of masters who define the possibilities of literature that belongs to the present. In most cases, if a political concern enters into the process of literary production—that is to say, if it enters into it at all, which is to say, rarely!—it is either through a guild model of apprenticeship or, more often, as a highly idiosyncratic expression of "style" (i.e., the work is valued to be "political," but *despite* the fact that the writer is black, a woman, a minority or ethnic subject, etc.). In place of a major form of literary history, what I might call the "dispositif" of the literary prize has emerged as the primary mechanism for producing "outstanding talent" and "major authors" who serve today as the fulcrum of the contemporary literary machine. In other words, in the publishing regime of creative writing, the literary prize replaces the relationship between the writer and the public, and the criterion of natural genius becomes an object of discipline and mass marketing. Here the people are missing, but in a completely different manner than was signaled by the earlier sense of the refrain, because their absence is never seen as a problem of what constitutes good writing, and mostly because the public is largely a patchwork made up of writers and their agents and publishers. In short, the creative writing workshop has become a factory.

On the other hand, what has happened to the question of minor literature in the critical theory classroom? Given that we have confirmed that most critical programs of interpretation today are also based on political slogans, which determine the selection of authors and writers employed as exemplary texts for political interpretation, does this recover at least some relation to the "liveliness" that Kafka associated with the culture of cafés and societies he frequented in Prague? Not exactly. Although the liveliness of polemics certainly exists in the society of critics, it never occurs in the full light of day, but rather, once again according to Kafka's fine phrase, in "the not indispensable cellar of a structure" that is established by the major forms of political interpretation. As a result, the politics of writers remains buried deep in the cellar of the structures erected by contemporary critics. In place of the petty and personal polemics that often inform the politics of writers, what determines the developments in form and "craft" is covered over by a style of "grand politics" that belongs to the various major regimes of political interpretation (e.g., Marxist, feminist, postcolonial, minority, queer, etc.).

In light of the above observations, perhaps it is past time to ask whether minor literature exists today. However, this question is already secondary to a more fundamental question that is seldom asked either by contemporary critics or by writers themselves (except, perhaps, in moments of loneliness and despair), which is the question of whether there is still something called literature today. Of course, this question seems laughable, since there are obviously generic forms of "creative writing" such as novels, poems, dramatic works, short stories, and so forth. But are these examples of "LITERATURE" in the sense that the concept had been previously employed to represent a national culture, a popular culture, a Republic of Letters, a literature of commitment, or even a minor literature? If we recall the definition given earlier by Roland Barthes—"literature is what is taught, period"—then it would behoove us to make a census of what is being taught today in departments of literature and in what manner this teaching matter is defined regarding the moral and civic values of the nation, especially in view of "small nations" or politically underrepresented minorities.

As an experiment, we might apply Kafka's description of the culture of minor writing rigorously and do the following ethnographic exercise. For example, we might choose to visit the monthly reading group or poetry reading in our local independent bookstore (which still exists in a run-down storefront of a former main street, now a racialized zone of the town or city) and survey current aesthetic and political slogans: feminism, race, queer or transgender identity, ecology, political diatribe, global economics, neoliberal society, and so forth. The difference between how these slogans might appear in the amateurish space of the local reading group and how they function as "order-words" when linked to the official function of teaching in the university or disciplinary context would be significant; the theme of politics would not need to be established by a structural or major form of political interpretation but would by justified by a spontaneous feeling, a mood, an individual or personal concern. In other words, "politics" would not need to take a scientific, epistemological, or didactic form in order to be justified. It would only take the form of a quasi-spontaneous expression of a feeling, whatever vehicle the individual writer uses to express the reality of this feeling, mood, affect, opinion, political concern, and so forth. Of course, the nature of this expression is usually a clichéd and highly derivative literary enunciation, which is why these local spaces are prejudged as informal and "amateurish"—ironically, the same judgments that Kafka determined as belonging to the conditions of minor literature. Perhaps this is why what is called "LITERATURE," minor or otherwise, is never expected to exist in local cafés and reading groups or in small journals and poetry magazines, and why these spaces exist either in a nostalgic form of literary community or, today, mostly in blogs and informal chat rooms.

As a result of the fact that what is called "literature" exists today only in universities, whether in the critical theory classroom or the creative writing workshop, the petty polemics and personal politics constituting the real social space in the disciplines of writing and literature assume patently ideological form of polemics between structures in which "the people" have actually become, according to Deleuze and Guattari's own premonition, "*a cardboard or paper people*." Here I believe we have uncovered a fourth, much more critical sense of the refrain: if the people are missing today it is because the reality of the people's concern has undergone repression and is now hidden by the major structures of power and judgment erected to represent their concerns. On this point I am in complete agreement with Rancière when he says that anytime one searches for the hidden beneath the apparent, a position of mastery is established.[1] It thus might be long overdue to challenge the tribunal of "political interpretation" that has prejudiced the apparent personal concerns of literature for more than half a century now. As one consequence, we could say that the people are not missing as much as they have simply been forgotten somewhere along the way, owing either to gross neglect or, in some cases, to intentional malevolence on the part of critics and writers themselves, or, in the most optimistic conclusion, merely to simple forgetfulness. In any case, *it is evident that the entire question of literature today, including so-called minor literature, is no longer the concern of any "people," either living or dead.*

As a result of this sorry state of affairs, I now turn to raise the following question: What is the responsibility of the contemporary writer and critic for the fact that the people are missing? Of course, this question alludes to the modern relationship installed by the Kantian phrase of ethical duty: "What ought we to do?" In other words, what is the ethical duty of the writer and critic today? In his last public remarks, Deleuze turns to the creative act itself that lies at the basis of both the work of art and the concept of philosophy and provides a simple definition of this duty: the work of art is an act of resistance. But resistance to what or to whom? According to well-known statements concerning the identity of the major adversaries Deleuze has in mind, we might say resistance to power, its various dispositifs, and to "systems of majority." Although this seems self-evident, it is also tautological. Why resist these when this is the only location of power itself, assuming that power only functions through its dispositifs, just as politics only flows through systems of majority, not only in democratic politics but also in the economic systems of majority operated by late capitalism? In discerning these powers, shouldn't the political critic, in particular, seek in some way to seize control of these same dispositifs and the systems of majority, if only to revolutionize them in direct support of those people who are most oppressed by these systems? Would this not be, ultimately, an act of resistance, according to a grand style of political interpretation?

Nevertheless, as we all know, the nature of the act that would be required to seize the dispositifs of cultural production is already presumed to be *too large* for either the academic critic or his or her contemporary surrogates (the cultural theorist, the independent creator, the agitprop artist, etc.). Moreover, as I observed above, the location of the contemporary critic is quite remote from these powerful dispositifs of art and culture, at the furthest point of periphery, in the contemporary research university. As one consequence, the revolutionary idea represents an intensive magnitude that is *too large, too powerful* for the critic to imagine, and it is this overpowering weakness of the critical imagination that is one figure of our contemporary sublime; the very fact that we can still imagine its possibility, even in a negative form, is the manner in which this idea has a reality, even though this reality cannot be effectuated by any contemporary subject of politics. It is for this reason that much contemporary political philosophy has substituted for the goal of practical action a negative form of transcendence—a negative theology, negative community, political theology, politics of immanence—or has even assumed a millennial and apocalyptic narrative of Universal History that is favored by Marxists and political theologians alike.

In many ways, Deleuze anticipated the situation I have just described in his earlier statement concerning the loss of the revolutionary goal of mass art forms: "If the people are missing, if there is no longer consciousness, evolution or revolution, it is the scheme of reversal which itself becomes impossible. There will no longer be conquest of power by a proletariat, or by a united or unified people."[2] What is worse is that, today, both artists and political critics already have a sentiment that if the revolution were to come—which is not likely—the people will not be on their sides, especially the global poor who are prone to become a little too fanatical and religious! This has become a source of resentment that has served to isolate the creators more, who now live walled up in their cosmopolitan compounds. In the case of the political aspirations of critics, they have become a little bit religious with their turn to political theology to shore up the ruins against the coming catastrophe. (One can often hear the strange and haunting melody of the ghost dances for literature being performed in English departments across the United States today.) Moreover, it is the same feeling of impossibility that determines the conditions of post-revolutionary art and philosophy in the West that has become strangely universalized and no longer pertains either to any particular minorities or to the future of "small nations," including those nations that continue to emerge in Eastern Europe today (where one might think the political vocation of minor literature might have a second life). Nevertheless, it appears that it is only from the perspective of the first-world philosopher that the impossibility of both art and community has become a universal refrain—*this is the time "We" live today!*

Concerning this feeling of impossibility, let us return once more to the refrain that reappears in the context of *Cinema 2*, where Deleuze offers a much more sobering assessment of the potential of revolutionary art—and just ten years after the revolutionary potential that was assigned to the same refrain in the conception of minor literature! Once again, in his analysis of the revolutionary conditions of modern political cinema, this potential has been relocated to the periphery, such that only third-world directors and oppressed minorities would have any access to the revolutionary conditions of art—*henceforth, only real minorities and the oppressed have the right to claim "the people are missing"!* Why is this so? According to Deleuze, this is because today any real revolutionary potential is now completely hidden from "western writers and directors by new mechanisms of power and systems of majority."[3] He continues:

> This acknowledgment of a people who are missing is not a renunciation of political cinema, but on the contrary the new basis on which it is founded, *in the third world and for minorities* [but this would also imply that political cinema is not *for* first-world critics!]. Art, and especially cinematographic art, must take part in this task: not that of addressing a people, which is presupposed to be already there, but of contributing to the invention of a people. The moment the master, or the colonizer, proclaims "there have never been people here," the missing people are a becoming, they invent themselves, in shanty towns and camps, or in ghettos, in new conditions of struggle to which necessarily political art must contribute.[4]

Again, we might wonder what happened in the short ten-year period to the revolutionary potential of minor literature as a universal aspiration. Why this "narrowing" and "isolation" of the revolutionary vision only to the cinema of minorities or to the cramped, mostly urban spaces of the "third world"? There is no real explanation offered in Deleuze's account. It is simply declared that in just a space of ten years the real conditions of political cinema now exist "only in the third world and only for minorities who now belong to the intolerable conditions that can define a missing people."[5] Maryvonne Saison addresses this crucial transition in the following passage, which I will quote at length:

The context of regional struggles leads however to the contradiction that one actually encounters between the plurality of minorities and the utopian unity of a fraternal community, between the multiplication of peoples and the idea of a missing people as a regulative political idea of the value of the minority. We can see this difficulty in a comment by Deleuze that follows the moment he envisions the consequences of abandoning the "consciousness, evolution, revolution" sequence [quoted earlier], this essential schema of reversal in the context of the classical cinema: "The death knell for consciousness-raising was precisely the consciousness that there was no people, but always several peoples, an infinity of peoples, who remained to be united, or should not be united, in order for the problem to change. It is in this way that third-world cinema is a cinema of minorities, because the people exist only in the condition of minority, which is why they are missing. It is in minorities that private business is immediately political." The identification of the private with the political has to do with its localization within minorities and the prospect of passing from the plurality of peoples to the singularity of a people no longer seems self-evident. How can we reconcile the idea that the people only exist in a state of minority, the plurality of minorities and peoples, *and the value attached to the invention of an absent people?*[6]

In response to this claim, however, I would argue that art can undoubtedly invoke an absent or missing people but is not capable of inventing one. Nevertheless, it seems that over the past thirty years many literary and film critics have accepted this as the objective of political interpretation—that is, to invent an absent people, rather than find a missing people—and have set off in expeditions through the cramped urban districts of the formerly third world to mine the new *glocal* conditions of political cinema and their anonymous mediators (in Cairo, Baghdad, New Delhi, Algiers, Morocco, Palestine, Mexico City, San Paulo, Busan, and Seoul). Nevertheless, over the same period these very conditions have gradually disappeared, as "contemporary world cinema" has emerged to comprise a global distribution of international markets and annual film festivals that produce, in wave after wave, new regional creators as well as new minority mediators between local center and global periphery.

More recently, some postcolonial critics have even claimed that the people never really existed to begin with, but were merely invented by Western critics who simply fabricated their own imaginary mediators that emerged from these cramped spaces, but only to satisfy a growing market demand for fresh representations of their own intolerable conditions. (For example, how many times must we sit through another lecture on the *Battle of Algiers*, pretending it has any relevance for depicting the "intolerable conditions" of Africa today?) Finally, as the last stage in this dialectical progression between center and periphery, it seems that everyone has become a little bored with the earlier genre of political cinema. In fact, some of political cinema's former mediators have moved to Hollywood in order to direct the next blockbuster, science fiction, or zombie film. Should this be so surprising in the age of global cinema? After all, has not the contemporary zombie film become a favored genre for depicting the intolerable conditions of the global poor, as well as a warning of the growing threat they now pose for the developing world? In a strange way, doesn't this also fit with Deleuze's description of the future political cinema—a cinema of "trance or crisis"?[7]

5

The Weakness of the Moral Analogy

Let's return now to address the moral analogy implied in the idea of the resistance as an artistic act that can no longer assume a "major form" in the postmodern context where mass art forms have subscribed to the universals of communication global marketing. Employing Foucault's analysis regarding the decline and absorption of political cinema by global markets (at least from the perspective of cultural production in Western societies), Deleuze claims that the conditions of collective enunciation are now hidden by "the mechanisms of power and systems of majority."[1] Once again, we should pay attention to the fact that this statement occurs in the context of the previous statements concerning precisely the organic impossibility of political art that were outlined a few years earlier in *Cinema 1*.

The major statement, "the act of art is a form of resistance," occurs in a rare public talk by a philosopher at the end of his life who barely has the strength to speak without great effort, almost whispering, that the act of art is resistance is repeated in his lecture more than thirty times.[2] In one sense, this could be heard as the philosopher's cry, in the same sense he ascribes to the statements of other philosophers, as in the case of the famous statement by Leibniz: "the real is rational." So, in attending to this statement, we should listen to the cry that can barely be heard over the straining of the exhausted lungs to take their next breath of air. Deleuze asks: "What relationship is there between the work of art and communication?" Answer: "None at all. A work of art is not an instrument of communication. A work of art has nothing to do with communication. A work of art does not contain the least bit of information. In contrast, there is a fundamental affinity between a work of art and an act of resistance. It has something to do with information and communication as an act of resistance."[3]

At this point, I will pause around this statement and make the following observations. To begin, the act of art is determined from the position of the "act," placing the "creative act" on the same level as the "political act" (i.e., an "act of resistance"). The latter is determined as practical action, which has action both as its subject matter and as an object of deliberate reflection "on how the subject ought to act" in a given situation and after successful deliberation usually authorizes the subject to *act*, or moves others to *act* on the situation. After sufficient deliberation has taken place over time and among different subjects in the same community, the agency that authorizes the action assumes the form of law, at which point the moments of reflection and deliberation can sometimes appear to take place mechanically. For example, in the situation of approaching an intersection in my car, it is a lawful action to take a left turn at the intersection when there is a green arrow; I am able to take a left turn, and thus I take the turn. There is little deliberation or reflection that goes into this act. I just do it because *I am able to . . . I am in the right . . . I make the turn.* It is this capacity or power that is possessed by the subject that assumes the legal form of consensus.

But how can this form of practical action first be applied to an act of resistance—and then only by analogy—to an act of creation in imagination or art (for the sake of convenience, "the act of art")? In the first case, there is a form of contingency that occurs within the practical subject of will; in the second, there is a heteronomy between the practical subject and the aesthetic subject of the act. (Lyotard would call this heteronomy the instance of a *differend* between two heterogeneous phrase regimes, which I will return to discuss in detail below.) The first occurs because the act cannot be deduced from the law that represents the consensus between subjects; it is not complete (i.e., it cannot predict, much less include, all future situations and all subjects), nor does it assume the form of mechanical causality (of cause and effect), which is responsible for of all "accidents" in the practical field of intersections.

Nevertheless, as Kant argued (just as Spinoza did earlier in the *Theologico-Political Treatise*), the faculty of reason often borrows from natural law an image of sovereignty to determine all occasions for all subjects as the maximal extension of its own ideas. This is a misrepresentation that frequently occurs in invoking the meaning of "the universal" and what Kant calls a transcendental illusion that is endemic to the representation of sovereign reason, which is the basis of the critique of practical reason. In fact, the only thing that can be deduced is the law's contingency in view of the autonomy of the subject of will (freedom). It is this freedom and this contingency, however, that will become for Kant the very source of its obligating or constraining character, as well as the source of the moral feelings of duty and respect. In other words, I turn left when the green arrow appears out of a feeling of respect for the law, not because I am receiving commands from the traffic light, or because my action is simply an automatic function of the traffic laws, even though my action appears to be automated as if it is connected to some cause-effect series, or mechanical causality. For example, I can understand the law and still not obey it; and resistance is already made possible by the autonomy of freedom that Kant deduces from the contingency of the empirical law, the cause of which he must further deduce as an idea of reason.

As Lyotard explains in a crucial notice on Kant's transcendental deduction in *The Differend*, what first appears as a contradiction in this case becomes the decisive proof of freedom itself as an *a priori* idea:

> It is because he attempts this passage [i.e., Kant first attempted to deduce the moral law directly from the faculty of cognition, as if it were a causality within a series of causes and effects] that he discovers its impossibility, that he ascertains that the moral law is not arrived at by deduction, and that he concludes that freedom is the cognitive monster, an originary form of causality.[4]

Perhaps it is around this cognitive monstrosity that we also might understand the significance of Deleuze's claim that *the act of art is (equal to) an act of resistance*. By linking the practical subject of will to the aesthetic subject of the creative act, Deleuze surreptitiously introduces an ethical deduction of a feeling that is comparable to the moral feelings of obligation and respect, namely, *the feeling of a moral duty*. Nonetheless, as in the case of Kant's moral analogy, the source of this feeling remains mysterious, even though it appears as a power that is both the condition and the limit of the subject's own feeling of autonomy and freedom. For Kant, the source of this feeling of obligation to the moral law is the subject of "Humanity," which is not a being of Reason, nor an "empty concept," but stands for a community of persons (one that cannot be represented by any historical or anthropological entity. since it is merely a "fiction" employed by the faculty of the understanding to represent the maximal extension of practical reasonable beings). According to this moral analogy, Deleuze's transposition of the ethical duty of the artist—*you ought to resist in representing the act of creating art*—can be rephrased as *you are obligated to act out of a feeling of respect and even duty to a missing people.*

In other words, Deleuze translates this moral feeling of obligation as resistance; however, *he fails to account for the actual source of this feeling or account for how it emerges in the sensible condition of the act of creation.* It is simply declared that there is a homology between acts: x = y, to create = to resist. It is at this point that we should discover that an error has been committed in the transcendental deduction. Nevertheless, on Deleuze's part this error should be understood as strategic or practical, that is to say, purposeful, willed, constructive, and in the final account a purely "political" solution to the groundless problem of the moral analogy. (After all, do not Deleuze and Guattari also claim that *there are no metaphors?*) Of course, this is not the first time Deleuze has resorted to changing the rules of a particular philosopher's system to his own advantages—especially, in the case of Kant, his professed "enemy"—in order to extend the game a little further, but especially for new possibilities and new resources for the "revolutionary" potential of art and philosophy. However, even in the context of the final statement, Deleuze also confesses his failure to account for the source of the analogy with the following question: "What is this mysterious relationship between a work of art and an act of resistance when the men and women who resist neither have the time nor sometimes the culture necessary to have the slightest connection with art? I do not know." Therefore, "the people are missing, and yet, at the same time, they are not missing."[5] In other words, the very fact that the people are missing means that the assumed fundamental affinity between a work of art and the idea of "a people" does not yet exist in the present, and in fact may never exist as a concept of the understanding, nor even as a consistent object of political interpretation. And yet "there is no work of art that does not call on a people who does not yet exist."[6] This is the strange paradox that only exists as a result of the creative act, which already assumes a certain homology with the idea of moral law, and with the idea of culture itself to assume the power of finality, that is, *the power to assign its own ends*.

At this point I want to underscore the homology that Deleuze establishes between the pure subject of will and the subject of creation. Thus, the act of creation is not compared to the act of resistance (i.e., creating is *like* resisting). In the passage established between the ethical phrase and the aesthetic phrase, there is not even the fictional device that is employed in the Kantian "as if" (*als ob*)—that is, create *as if* you were also resisting. Instead, he simply declares that there is a relation of identity between the act of resisting and the act of art, even though the relationship remains mysterious, given that it is not an object of cognition or understanding (which are excluded *a priori*) but rather a pure affect or intensive feeling that cannot be deduced in the same way as the Kantian ethical deduction of the categorical imperative. Earlier on, I referred to this relationship between the subject of practical action and the subject of aesthetic creation by the name of heteronomy, since the source of the act is unfathomable and I can employ only symbols to represent the autonomy of freedom that lies at the basis of both acts. In other words, my freedom to create, like my freedom to resist, remains unfathomable and, in some ways, groundless. If I cannot deduce this freedom from a law, the question remains concerning how the freedom of the creative act can be deduced at all without turning it back into an abstraction. (In some ways, this is equal to the problem of creation, the creative act, since I can only know it after the fact!) Kant's invocation of "Humanity" (as the maximal extension of reasonable beings) as the mysterious source of my moral obligation is, in some ways, no different from Deleuze's invocation of a people as the source of the artist's ethical obligation, or to put this more simply in the terms of

Deleuze and Guattari's concept of "minor literature," the source of the writer's political concern (i.e., "the people's concern is necessarily political"). However, it is the exact nature of this homology that we must now try to resolve by adding a process of deduction back into Deleuze's elliptical claim that "the act of creation is an act of resistance."[7]

To begin the process of our deduction, it is clear that there is a *moral feeling* at the basis of the obligation to create a political artwork, a feeling that might, upon first glance, resemble the more elevated and ethical senses of "duty" or "respect." Of course, this mysterious feeling of "duty" has been interpreted in different ways and according to very different "phrase regimens," to again employ Lyotard's terminology. For example, it is this feeling of ethical duty that was the basis of Sartre's earlier definition of "the literature of commitment" (*l'arte engagé*), which became the subject of intense controversy in the postmodern tradition of political interpretation that followed. However, without this *a priori* analogy, the idea of the creative act would never appear as a supplement to the sphere of practical actions, especially when the subject of practical action is faced with the idea of an act that is too large or impossible to realize under its own powers, producing a feeling of pain that in some way can be compared to the negative feeling of the sublime. Before going any further in our deduction, however, it is crucial to observe that the origin of this feeling was a fundamental problem that intensely preoccupied both Deleuze and Lyotard at the end of their philosophical careers. Moreover, it is extremely significant that both turned to Kant's *Third Critique* in order to address this passage between politics and aesthetics.

Therefore, first let's examine Lyotard's approach to this passage. According to the many descriptions offered in *The Differend*, the ethical phrase is essentially constituted by two distinct voices: the addressor instance and the addressee instance.

The addressor instance is the voice of obligation (which comes to be occupied by reason, morality, law), and the addressee instance, which is not the subject but rather the voice of conscience, the friend, society, the people, the Other (*Autrui*), whatever name one wants to ascribe to this internal voice whose source remains mysterious in every sense. To quote Lyotard: "In 'hearing' *You ought to*, the addressee would at the same time 'hear' a phrase to which he or she cannot attest, but which is, as it were, awaiting its formulation under his or her responsibility and which would be *You are able to*."[8] In this regard, it is a bit like the scene of Elisha and Elijah in the darkened room: Elisha hears a voice and mistakes it for the voice of Elijah, when it is in fact God or his archangel who is speaking. As Lyotard concludes, the question put to critical metalanguage is knowing whether the *you* in "*You ought to* and the you in *You are able to* are the same you."[9] Thus, the homology between these two voices constitutes the subject of the practical action, which is thereby brought into a harmony with its own principle.

However, this mysterious attribution reveals the very anachronism at the source of the analogy itself: in the moral situation, the obligating phrase comes first but is expressed in a voice that always remains silent, representing a spontaneous and active power of law that authorizes the act. In other words, the phrase "I am able to" actually represents the completion of the action, or *the objective consensus of action with the principle of law*. For example, the green arrow says "you ought to turn left" and, at the same time, "you are able to turn left"; *ergo, I turn left*. On the other hand, what is invoked in the phrase of freedom is actually the spontaneous consensus of the act with an indeterminate law, which is not a problem of power in the sense of eventuality or causality but rather in the sense of the spontaneous ability to act prior to the law, that is to say, *the ability to become the first cause in a series that includes principle, obligation, and action within one duration*.

What is resistance then, according to this scheme? For Lyotard, resistance is nothing except the freedom enacted in the refusal to link action onto the obligation, since "the content of the command would be empirical and the manner of linking onto to the command would be contingent."[10] Thus, freedom represents the refusal of consensus with the moral voice, which opens the "I am able to" to becoming first in a new series, or to the phrasing of a new obligation, since the "I am able to" appears as a power that is equal to the "You ought to" (i.e., the command phrase) and is equally spontaneous or "free" (meaning not predetermined by causality). In other words, the phrase "I am able to" expresses a power that inaugurates an entirely new causal series and which then must await the consensus of a new addressee, which for both Kant and Lyotard (although not for Deleuze, as we will soon see) is a third party who judges the action and whose agreement represents the genesis of a new *sensus communis*. This condition of genesis resembles the emergence of judgment in a common-law tradition via the "matter of first impression," which must finally await the consensus of future judgments in order to become law by means of a process of accretion.

Now, it is precisely in this moment that we can glimpse the relation to the aesthetic act, since it is in this mysterious passage from the moral sphere of practical action to the aesthetic sphere of the creative act that a strange reversal takes place: in the creative act the "I am able to" phrase actually precedes the "You ought to" phrase, thereby introducing a fundamental dissymmetry between the two phrases and their historical-juridical representatives. Consequently, what I have called "heteronomy" is what Deleuze calls "resistance" and what Lyotard calls "the *differend*," and more recently what Rancière names "dissensus." This event represents the spontaneous power accorded to the act of art which fundamentally reverses the coordinates of the faculties for governing the practical subject of action, which is why the aesthetic field in modernity suddenly becomes a juridical and moral problem to resolve, since the "I am able to" of certain rare artistic acts cannot be determined by any form of causality other than that of the freedom of the will coming into harmony with itself *as if* in conformity with its own law. *In a nutshell, this is why the act of art becomes a powerful symbol of the freedom of political expression from the artistic period of modernism onward.*

Of course, as is well documented, Kant already had a presentiment of the symbolic capacity of aesthetic experience in the *Critique of the Power of Judgment*, where he first attempted to deduce the free and "spontaneous" and "universal" judgment of taste as an analogue to the subjective autonomy of freedom, which will henceforth provide a powerful symbolic analogy to the artwork from the period of Romanticism onward. Nevertheless, the conditions of this analogy between moral and aesthetic experience must first be prepared by installing the passage between these two domains, which Kant himself did not successfully accomplish in the last part on the teleology of History and, as a result, has set the mark for much of the aesthetic philosophy that followed, especially in the twentieth century. In the case of the moral idea of revolutionary action, for example, which was an object of reflection and contemplation in the Kantian determination of a sublime feeling of enthusiasm, this "negative feeling" has been consigned to the aesthetic field in a narrow, limited, or symbolic sense, which is often colored by the affective moods of melancholia (Benjamin), the failure or impossibility of the act (Bataille, Blanchot), its purely virtual event (Badiou), or, finally, by its disguise or displacement in the aesthetic act (Deleuze, Rancière). In the case of Deleuze and Guattari's concept of "minor literature," this last permutation can be perfectly illustrated by recalling the major definition of the conditions of the "literary machine," which becomes the relay for a revolutionary machine-to-come, because the literary machine is determined to fill the conditions of a collective enunciation that is lacking in other spheres of practical activity. Elsewhere, including the last statements on art, Deleuze always adds a line of force leading directly to the outside, like a great wind that gathers up all the elements and carries them into the future but in the form of pure anticipation or "revolutionary becoming."

At the same time, we must not imagine that the creative act alone is sufficient to establish this analogy, which is why Kant also chooses to locate the subject of judgment in the position of the public spectator rather than from the perspective of the artist or creator (or natural genius). It is in this place that the historical-juridical persona of the critic as the official spokesperson of "the public" will also be located in the extension of the creative act, both in terms of "openness" (*Öffentlichkeit*) and in its quantitative degree of objectivity. In other words, no creative act is complete in its own presentation (*Darstellung*) until the full extension of this presentation encompasses the position of a spectator, the public, a community of persons, or a virtual community of reasonable beings (i.e., a people, a Humanity) that conditions the very "openness" of a *sensus communis* (i.e., communal sensibility, *gemeinschaftlichen Sinn*). It is here we find the most critical observation by Lyotard: in the feeling of universality that belongs to aesthetic imagination, the imagination is not a power that is equal to the most general "object = x," but only a "field" (*champ*) that is determined in the form of reflective judgment, which is a reflective act and not a creative act, *since for Kant there can be no act of judgment without concepts!* As Kant puts it: "For while intuitions can be sensible, judging pertains to absolutely nothing but the understanding in the broadest meaning of the term."[11] Consequently, as Lyotard concludes, *there will never be a direct presentation of the idea of community in an aesthetic presentation*, but rather only an indirect presentation, since there are no concepts of the understanding, merely symbols.[12]

Kant already foreshadowed the transcendental function of schematism in *The Critique of Pure Reason*, where reflective judgment is effected by the faculty of the imagination under the power of the understanding, which must first "compose" the "field" of sensibility into a frame or "monogram, of pure *a priori* imagination" (A142/B181).[13] Kant further describes this monogram as an "'outline' [*Umriß*], a 'sketch' [*Zeichnung*], or a 'silhouette' [*Schattenbild*] of an object" (A833/B862 and A570/B598).[14] Therefore, it is the "reflective" nature of the synthesis performed by the artwork that underlies the distinction between the aesthetic composition of a "field" of sensation and the *a priori* schematization of conditions of space and time.[15]

As Kant defines the role of schemata in the first *Critique*, in order for us to be able to apply a concept to an intuition, "it is clear that there must be a third thing [*ein Drittes*], which must stand in homogeneity [*Gleichartigkeit*] with the category on the one hand and the appearance on the other, and makes possible the application of the former to the latter. This mediating representation must be . . . *intellectual* on the one hand and *sensible* on the other. Such a representation is the *transcendental schema*" (A138/B177). In the comparison to *Kunst*, which is later defined exclusively as the production through freedom (i.e., "a capacity for choice that grounds its actions in reason"), "the imagination's ability to make a concept sensible is just that, an ability (*Können*): it involves skills that outstrip our theoretical knowledge (*Wissen*)."[16] Thus, Kant further distinguishes between artistic skill and science: "*Kunst* as a skill [*Geschicklichkeit*] of human beings is also distinguished from science [*Wissenschaft*] (*to be able* from *to know* [*Können vom Wissen*]), as a practical faculty from a theoretical one, as technique [*Technik*] from theory" (κυ 5:303). In other words, the second synthesis performed by the imagination already presupposes a "sensible frame," which is the composition of a certain space and a certain time by means of which diversity is related to the object in general (i.e., "object = x") in conformity with the categories. Thus, the schema is a spatiotemporal determination that corresponds to the categories; *it does not consist in any image per se but rather is composed of (or composes) spatiotemporal relations that are purely conceptual.* On the other hand, the source of art's technical ability to create a spontaneous analogy between the moral idea and the sensible field does not constitute a knowledge arrived at through concepts, but rather through its ability to fashion symbols (i.e., indirect presentations).

Nevertheless, in establishing the symbolized object (in this case, the supersensible object of the moral law) and the symbolizing object (in this case, the aesthetic presentation), both must remain in "utterly different" phrase universes, according to Lyotard.[17] Why? According to the Kantian understanding, this is because there can be no direct intuition of the supersensible idea of the moral law itself, given the definition of the moral law as a law of causality through freedom, that is to say, the spontaneity and the causality of the subject as a *thing in itself.* Since there can be no direct intuition of the transcendental Subject, this becomes the very condition of the symbolic to establish the passage of the ideas of reason into subjective experience, a symbol whose original figure refers to two broken halves or shards that will remain forever fragmentary even when they are fitted or pieced together. As Lyotard adds, "symbolization, then, does not occur through the substitution of objects, but through permutations of instances in the respective phrase universes, but without recourse to any direct presentation."[18]

Here, it is critical to notice that the very first descriptions of the mysterious art of schematism in the *Critique of Pure Reason* are already likened to a "'blurred sketch drawn from diverse experiences,' 'an incommunicable shadowing image [in painting],' or to a 'model' . . . which 'furnishes no rules that allow of being explained and examined.'"[19] In other words, all of these examples of the technique (*Kunst*) of the imagination to schematize are already derived from the empirical field of the artwork itself, and especially from the plastic arts as the genre of particular kinds of images. In all these examples, as Lyotard observes, "Kant turns this evanescent something or other into a creation of the imagination."[20] For example, Kant even compares them to the sketches that painters have in their heads (A57/B598).[21] One might conclude, therefore, that Kant's own analogy between cognitive and aesthetic form of *sensus communis* remains impure, that is to say, based upon the external resemblance to an empirical art form, especially painting, which changes according to historical and social laws, and not internally, or formally, according to its own genetic idea.

Moreover, this weak and patently empirical analogy is the basis for Kant's frequent description of Nature as "a great artist" and of schematism itself as a "hidden art" that could be comparable to the act of natural genius. In other words, the spontaneous and form-giving power that belongs to the creative act is already likened to the protean and prodigious power of nature; however, this analogy remains patently metaphorical, if not a simile, the weakest of symbols, since it is fashioned by mere external resemblance (i.e., nature is *like* an artist, the act of imagination is *like* the act of art, the art of schematism is *like* the creative art of the natural genius, etc.). Perhaps another way of describing this weak analogy is that it represents the danger of a transcendental illusion that is internal to the faculty of the imagination itself, which assumes a dominant role in the aesthetic presentation of the ideas of reason, and thus this illusion will become the basis of the critique of the faculty of the imagination. For example, in the feeling of universality that is presented in the ideas of the beautiful and the sublime, the imagination has no concept in order to present its intuition of what is essentially "an indeterminate and undeterminable" object (i.e., "object = x"), which is equal to the *a priori* conditions of time and space. Moreover, in the case of the aesthetic presentation of the idea of "the Whole," the maximal extension of the idea of community, the imagination extends beyond the realm of phenomena by means of the use of the power of schematism, but the danger of illusion consists in giving this idea the appearance of an objective reality, in reference to an existing "people," "nation," or even "race."

At this point I return to what I called earlier Deleuze's practical (i.e., political) solution to problem of the transcendental deduction of the moral analogy. In *Difference and Repetition*, five years after the publication of *Kant's Critical Philosophy* (1963), Deleuze attempts to resolve this passage by appealing to the principle of intensive quantities introduced by the Neo-Kantian Hermann Cohen, who attached full value to the principle of intensive quantities in his reinterpretation of Kant. Thus, Deleuze writes, "While space may be irreducible to concepts, its affinity with Ideas cannot nevertheless be denied"—in other words, its capacity (as *intensive spatium*) to determine in extension the actualization of ideal connections as differential relations virtually contained in the Idea. Therefore, "While the conditions of possible experience may be related to extension, there are also subjacent conditions of real experience which are indistinguishable from intensity as such."[22]

Perhaps in one of the most remarkable and singular resistances to the conditions of the passage that was first established by Kant, Deleuze's own solution from the very beginning of his philosophical project was to restore the conditions of the sensibility to the first synthesis effected by the power of the transcendental schematism. In *Difference and Repetition*, this transcendental condition of sensibility, equal to the "object = x," is thus called the "dark precursor," directly referring to Kant's blurred sketch, or the adumbrated image of the monogram noted above. And yet, like Kant, Deleuze derives this primitive symbol from the composition of the aesthetic field. Why is this so important? Because even earlier in Kant, this analogy was already presented negatively as an "ideal image of sensibility" and not, as established in the transcendental aesthetic, as the simple receptivity of the cognitive faculty.[23] For Kant, the act of an imagination is never actually free and unfettered, since it must find its action and its specific role already determined in conformity with the concepts of the understanding. Nevertheless, Deleuze cannot resist the temptation to idealize the conditions of artistic creation, albeit in certain rare and special cases, as actually having the power *to restore the transcendental empirical field of sensibility to an immanent form!* In other words, the act of creation gives us an immediate access to this sensible field in-itself, or in Kantian terms, the act of art represents a power that gives us the possibility of a direct intuition without concepts of the understanding. Thus, in certain rare and special occasions, or in the case of certain exceptional individuals, the creation of art is not *subject to* the faculty of the understanding! "In fact," Deleuze argues, "the imagination does something other than schematize: it displays its deepest freedom in reflecting the form of the object, it is 'as it were, in general at play in the contemplation of the figure.'"[24]

Deleuze had foreseen the path to this solution as early as the 1963 discussion of the sublime, where he writes, "The analysis of the sublime has set us on the right track, since it showed us a common sense which was *not merely assumed, but engendered.*"[25]

Here, the act of art becomes a purely productive and spontaneous imagination, requiring no previous synthesis of the imagination as a general faculty, but rather, according to the new definition offered by Deleuze from this point onward, liberated from the legislative role of the understanding to become the source of "arbitrary forms of possible intuitions."[26] Another way of saying this is that the act of art now provides the real conditions of sensible experience and not just the objects of possible experience for the understanding. In turn, this will become a major refrain in Deleuze's philosophy from *Proust and Signs* onward: "real without being actual, ideal without being abstract."[27]

To illustrate this further I could quote any number of passages from Deleuze's philosophy, all of which can be seen as variations of the same ideal solution: *that the act of art can actually restore sensibility to an immanent plane and thus to an act that might resemble a pure sense of a faculty in the Kantian sense, which is to say, a pure and impersonal "being of sensation."* Moreover, this reduction is what distinguishes what is called a "percept" from perception and the "affect" from emotion in the last work written with Guattari. In all of these examples, however, what is subtracted is the Subject, which restores the being of sensation to a plane of immanence, forming monuments of sensation that no longer need a subject to see or feel, since everything is reduced to pure vision and feeling: "*Affects are precisely these nonhuman becomings of man*, just as percepts ... are *nonhuman landscapes of nature*." As Deleuze and Guattari quote the enigmatic statement by Cézanne, "Man absent from but entirely within the landscape."[28]

What is first presented in Kant as an ideal or speculative leap of the imagination that is only limited by the power of reason itself, in Deleuze becomes an actual leap that is performed by the act of art in order to create an image of our "supersensible destination" (albeit in a negative form that is reflected in the experience of the sublime) "so that, in the dynamic sublime, the supersensible destination of our faculties appears as *that to which our moral being is predestined.*"[29] For Deleuze, this solution provides the reverse proof of the passage between the aesthetic form of common sense to the genesis of a new moral common sense; however, this must be understood not in the sense of creating a "new people," which, Deleuze and Guattari say elsewhere, would be comparable to science fiction. Instead, it is simply assumed that the act of art, in certain rare and extraordinary cases, can provide us the passage to the genesis (literally, the engenderment) of a new *sensus communis*, a new "communal sensibility," which is not restricted or limited to a highly "individuated form," such as the ideal of the imagination that occurs in the creative act of natural genius, as it was in Kant. Therefore, what Kant only saw as "an ideal synthesis" of the imagination, which schematizes without being guided by either the concepts of the understanding or the idea of reason, Deleuze will now claim as the "real condition" of the artwork, even though the actualization of this condition must be limited to small list of artists, writers, and musicians who supplant the natural role of genius in Kant. In comparison with the figure of natural genius, which for Kant represents the ideal synthesis of the faculty of the imagination with the creative act, the faculty of the understanding still maintains an important role as a critical limit in complete extension of the schematism effected through the creative act, a limit that is embodied in the first determination of *sensus communis* understood as a quasi-object that must be common to all three faculties.[30]

According to Kant's view, genius is an original talent for producing a work for which no determinate rule can be given, and since the artist's own talent must give the rule to art, then "originality must be the primary characteristic [of natural genius]" (KU 5:307–8). Nevertheless, for Kant, genius must also first involve "a relation of the imagination to the understanding"

(KU 5:317), if only because "if the artist's activity does not involve this cooperation between the imagination and understanding, then the artist will produce 'nonsense,' rather than a work of art that can become 'exemplary' to serve as a model for other artists."[31] In Deleuze's account, however, the role of the understanding has been demoted and the general faculty no longer furnishes concepts to guide the speculative labor of the imagination in schematizing the object in collaboration with the other faculties. This demotion is ultimately completed in the last book with Guattari, *What Is Philosophy?* Instead of the faculty of understanding providing concepts, here philosophy itself assumes this role, even though this act is now defined as essentially creative as well, since it is claimed that philosophy alone can "create concepts." In other words, on one side, in place of the faculty of understanding, we have the role of the philosopher, which is to create concepts under the condition that this is not a form of communication and has nothing to do with providing information or understanding according to the earlier sense of the role of the understanding. And on the other side, and in place of the faculty of imagination, art creates monuments that are like pure blocks of sensation, but under the condition that the creation of art also communicates nothing, since these monuments are pure compositions of sensation that want to "restore the infinite" (here, recalling the primary role of the transcendental schemata).[32] This is perfectly illustrated in Deleuze's talk on the act of creation with the description of Bresson's distinct type of space-time made up from little blocks of duration that have no predetermined connection.[33] The question then becomes, how does communication take place at all, even between the creative philosopher and creative artist? It is around this point that Deleuze again invokes the character of genius, and the impersonal and solitary figures of the philosopher and artist communicate across vast eternities:

"In the arts, the accord of imagination and understanding is brought to life only by genius, and without [which] it would remain incommunicable. Genius is a summons sent out to another genius; but taste becomes a sort of medium between the two [thus, subjective taste replaces common sense, since only genius can recognize genius], allowing a waiting period if the other genius is not yet born [i.e., I would immediately add, it is found to be "missing"]."[34]

The final solution is to preserve what remains of these monuments for eternity. The act of art is encased in a monument of sensation, which jettisons the subject of the artist as well. The artist becomes impersonal, just as the writer of minor literature becomes a bachelor, and the proper name now functions as an instantaneous apprehension of a multiplicity, echoing the first sense of the faculty of imagination enumerated above. Instead, the block of sensation is produced by certain function as transcendental scheme of space-time, which is why the artist must become impersonal, and the work itself a monument that is planted in the earth like a tree from another world. In Deleuze's last descriptions, all great art has this character of encasement and non-communication. The monument does not speak, does not give information, does not seek to communicate or translate its experience into the common world of opinion. "How can a moment of the world be rendered durable and made to exist by itself?"[35] This is the only remaining concern of the artist or the writers that Deleuze and Guattari choose in their last work: Cézanne, Goya, Van Gogh, "even Daumier and Redon"; Woolf, Miller, Melville, Beckett and Kafka; finally, directors like Bresson, Kurosawa, Straub, and Rossellini. The reply: "Saturate every atom" of the artwork, "eliminate all waste," until there is no longer anything left of our common sense (i.e., everything that adheres to our current and lived perceptions), much less any oxygen left to breathe.[36]

As a final point of comparison with Kant's original understanding of this passage—and, as we have seen, with Lyotard's as well—let us return to the mysterious source of the "feeling" of the universal agreement (*sensus communis universalis*). In the case of the feeling of the beautiful as a purely subjective assumption of universal judgment from the position of the spectator, the actual subject of agreement (or consensus) is assigned to the idea of a "Humanity," defined as the maximal extension of reasonable beings. However, this directly implies that the "universal agreement" never takes place in the present of the act of aesthetic judgment, but rather is permanently suspended in abeyance and must await an agreement by an unknown party to the judgment, *but with the permanent expectation that this consensus will finally bring the act of judgment into harmony with its own condition of possibility*. In this regard, there is homology established between the purely subjective principle of aesthetic judgment and the objective principle of the moral law, as Kant had established, since the idea of universal agreement (*sensus communis universalis*) can only assume a negative form of presentation in the present, since in both regions of lived experience no judgment can be final.

It is this tense and impatient expectation that has been at the center of most of the discussions of the importance of the sublime in determining that negative presentation of a new *sensus communis*, and even the possibility of the arrival of a new people that is invoked by the modern artwork. As Lyotard explains this form of anticipation, "It is this universality in abeyance or in suspense that is invoked by the aesthetic judgment . . . [but] this common or communal sense does that guarantee that 'everyone will agree with my judgment, but [only] that [they] *ought* [to].'"[37] For Deleuze and Guattari, on the other hand, the idea of sensible community is "minor," even non-democratic (as we will see), *and precisely this because the notion of "becoming minor" never seeks to obtain a form of a universal agreement.* Consequently, in their last work we find only the negative and pejorative sense of *sensus communis universalis* in the phrase "the universals of communication and marketing" that they assign to late capitalism and to global commodity culture (e.g., "universal markets"). As I noted above, if the *sensus communis* is already identified as a major form *de jure*, then any idea of resistance must always assume a minor form *de facto*. This constitutes an axiom for Deleuze, which is also the axiom of "becoming minor." As I have questioned elsewhere concerning the concept of a revolutionary people today, this leads to an impasse in the concept itself, since the minor can never assume the desire of becoming a majority and must never seek recognition as a "minority" by appealing to a principle of identity, since this recognition could only take place according to the terms of a majoritarian form.[38]

This rejection of the idea of *sensus communis* is symptomatic of Deleuze's long and steadfast "anti-Kantianism," which was dominant through his entire philosophical project, beginning with the early primer on Kant, where he intentionally transforms Kant's theory of the faculties in order to demote the role played by the faculty of the understanding in the *Critique of Judgment*. Above we have already discovered Deleuze's strategic elision of the faculty of the understanding, but more importantly the original role played by the character of "openness" and "publicity" that function as limiting factors of receptivity in the *Critique of Judgment*. Once again, the act of art can never complete its presentation alone, something I will return to in the following chapter around the original statement by Paul Klee from which Deleuze derives the second component of the refrain.

In place of the role of the "public," we have the isolation of the role assumed by the artist (in place of natural genius) in the act of creating a new communal being of sensibility that will belong to "the people who are missing or still to come." And it is for this reason that Deleuze's ideal concept of the "people" can never refer to a "Humanity" in the Kantian sense (nor even in the sense employed later by Lyotard). In fact, both terms must be understood as "forms of majority," which, according to a major axiom of Deleuze's philosophy, must either be resisted or eluded altogether through a creative process of "becoming minor." In short, this would be the ideal genesis of a new *sensus communis*, which would necessarily be a minor form *par excellence*. For example, if we simply survey Deleuze and Guattari's last work for the minor figure of this new *sensus communis*, it would be a minority composed of three groups: artists, who create percepts and affects; scientists and mathematicians, who create functions; and philosophers, who create concepts. It is around this ideal consensus that art and philosophy suddenly converge in the constitution of a new earth summoned forth by philosophy and a people yet to come as a correlate of solitary creation. Moreover, "it is not populist writers but the most aristocratic who lay claim to this future. This people and earth will not be found in our democracies. Democracies are majorities, but a becoming is by its nature that which always eludes the majority."[39]

Simply put, if the people are missing, it is because *le peuple* are the subject of a *faux ami*, a misnomer, from the very beginning. In other words, the entity of *le peuple* (in *le sens communautaire*) are not the *demos*. Thus, the coming people cannot be mistaken for any democratic concept of *demos*. In one sense, this is why Deleuze and Guattari's concept of minor literature has produced so much confusion when applied to actual minorities, since the only proper destination of a minority is to become more minor, and eventually to become imperceptible. Nevertheless, as Deleuze and Guattari also conclude, the powers of both philosophy and art today are limited; they can summon a people but cannot create them. In other words, the intolerable situation that was described in *Cinema 2* and was consigned to the abominable sufferings of the "third world" in their last book becomes the millennial conditions of both art and philosophy in the contemporary world, where they also say, inasmuch as the people can only be concerned with their own abominable suffering, they can't be concerned any longer with the future of art or philosophy.[40]

6

The Final Sense of the Refrain

It is at this point in our tracing the evolution of the refrain "the people are missing" that we bear witness to the loss of the revolutionary ideal that was clearly present in Deleuze's earlier works, which is eventually replaced by a tragic pessimism and even apocalyptic image of the people who are missing in the last writings that address the possibility of art as an act of resistance to the contemporary universals of communication and mass media. Of course, I realize I am exaggerating the eschatological sense of the refrain for dramatic effect, even though it can clearly be found in the later works as I have quoted in the earlier chapters. All of the above claims, including the earliest, are premised upon the revolutionary aspiration that art (or literature) is capable of engendering a new *sensus communis* in place of the universals of communication and culture. And yet, as we have seen, this claim is never established or proven to even be possible to begin with, and after the history of numerous failures accompanied by the feeling of intense betrayal that eventually comes to characterize the impossibility of both philosophy and art today.

To summarize the eschatological sense of the refrain, concerning the end times, in Deleuze's later philosophy we discover a strange blend of tragic Stoicism mixed with a Nietzschean aristocratic morality that was already present at the very beginning of his philosophical project. This is especially remarkable in the last work with Guattari, where we have the image of the noble philosopher-artist who withdraws into the garden at midnight to contemplate the twilight of the earth and to dream of a people who are missing. Deep in this thought, which plunges into the chaos that surrounds the contemporary moment, there emerges the shadow of "the people to come," as if the last image that Deleuze gives is the shadow of Eurydice as she turns away and descends back into the underworld. Therefore, the final sense of the refrain appears in the millennial summons of "a new earth and a new people." *Millennium* is from the Latin *mille*, "one thousand," and *annus*, "year"—hence the two *n*'s, whereas *millenarian* is from the Latin *millenarius*, "containing a thousand (of anything)," hence no *annus*, and only one *n*.[1] As Deleuze himself is clearly aware, the final sense of the refrain is made in an allusion to the following passage from the Apocalypse of John:

> 1. Then I saw "a new heaven and a new earth," for the first heaven and the first earth had passed away, and there was no longer any sea. 2. I saw the Holy City, the new Jerusalem, coming down out of heaven from God, prepared as a bride beautifully dressed for her husband. 3. And I heard a loud voice from the throne saying, "Look! God's dwelling place is now among the people, and he will dwell with them. They will be his people, and God himself will be with them and be their God. 4. 'He will wipe every tear from their eyes. There will be no more death' [b] or mourning or crying or pain, for the old order of things has passed away."

In his afterword to the French edition of "Bartleby, the Scrivener: A Story of Wall Street" (1989), Deleuze recasts this millenarian view of people who are missing (or yet to come) in a Melvillean jeremiad concerning the failure of the two great revolutionary societies of the nineteenth century: the American and the Soviet. In their origin, the revisionary hope is the fabrication of a "new human being" without particulars. In the case of the American revolution this is fashioned through universal immigration, the inmixing and gradual blending of all races and bloodlines into a new people that bears no particular origin or hereditary physiognomy, a society of bastards, castaways who become brothers, a fraternity of émigrés, and sisters without common property or consanguinity. "A brother, a sister, all the truer for no longer being 'his or 'hers,' since all 'property,' and 'proprietorship,' has disappeared."[2] In the case of the Soviet revolution, the universal society is achieved through the great modern scientific project of the socialization of man, which strips the masses of all particularities (race, ethnicity, family, religion, even sexual characteristics). Accordingly, the concept of the people can no longer correspond to its original natal form of the nation; the people are "created" (or rather, *produced by scientific materialism*) and thus no longer organically "born into" a family, a community, a *Volk* or "nation" (according to the eighteenth-century understanding of these terms).

However, both of these nineteenth-century utopian expressions of the "universal nation"—or what Deleuze calls the two heads of nineteenth-century messianism—already contain the seeds of failure, and their poisonous trees are firmly planted in the soil of each universal by the turn of the century, which prepares for the return of the paternal function that threatens to become even more violent and lawless because it now threatens the entire planet with total war. Thus, for Deleuze, the American Civil War already prefigured the failure of the Soviets to unify the society of brothers, and this becomes the importance of Melville as a great prophet of the twentieth century. It was a crack opened in the soil of the nation that was founded upon a fundamental and primitive division of racial and economic inequality, a crack that continued to widen throughout the nineteenth century until it connected with the archipelagoes of European colonialism and the capillaries of the class division, until the crack reached the planetary proportion of the universal division between rich and poor that neither cosmopolitanism nor Christian charity could any longer cover over or conceal. Even worse is the loss of the primitive confidence and respect this reintroduces in the paternal function itself, and its replacement by what Dionyse Mascolo has called a "generalized Machiavellianism."[3] Deleuze summarizes this danger in the following passage:

> The dangers of a "society without fathers" have often been pointed out, but the only real danger is the return of the father. In this respect, it is difficult to separate the failure of the two revolutions, the American and the Soviet, the pragmatic and the dialectical. Universal emigration was no more successful than universal proletarization. The Civil War already sounded the knell, as would the liquidation of the Soviets later on. The birth of a nation, the restoration of the nation-state—and the monstrous fathers come galloping back in, while the sons without fathers start dying off again. Paper images—this is the fate of the American as well as the Proletarian. But just as many Bolsheviks could hear the diabolical powers knocking at the door in 1917, the pragmatists, like Melville before them, could see the masquerade that the society of brothers would lead to.[4]

This passage is the full chapter and verse of Deleuze's prophecy concerning the ultimate failure of the American revolution specifically, which was betrayed by the horde of confidence men and carpetbaggers who rushed into the breach of American society following the Civil War to sell their lightning rods and snake oil to the mass of "*overly credulous* Americans." In this prophecy we also find the diagnosis of "our sick America" today, which speaks to the loss of the people's confidence in the democratic ideal of achieving any true equality between brothers, between brothers and sisters in the absence of a common father, and instead the return of a horde of brothers who appear to have pieced together the father's dead corpse into the monstrous body of the "universal nation-state." As Deleuze asks: "Are these false brothers sent by a diabolical father to restore his power over *overly credulous* Americans?"[5]

In reply, I quote a long passage in which Deleuze describes the bright peacock coat of this new sovereign made from a patchwork of Melville's stories:

> The great community of celibates is nothing more than a company of bons vivants, which certainly does not keep the rich bachelor from exploiting the poor and pallid workers, by reconstituting the two unreconciled figures of the monstrous father and the orphaned daughters (*The Paradise of Bachelors and the Tartarus of Maids*). The American confidence-man appears everywhere in Melville's work. What malignant power has turned the trust into a company as cruel as the abominable "universal nation" founded by the Dog-Man in *The Encantadas*? *The Confidence-Man*, in which Melville's critique of charity and philanthropy culminates, brings into play a series of devious characters who seem to emanate from a "great Cosmopolitan" in patchwork clothing, and who ask for no more than . . . a little human confidence, in order to pull off a multiple and rebounding confidence game.[6]

The above passage is pieced together from the characters of Melville like a new Leviathan that emerges at the end of the nineteenth century and continues to pick its teeth with broken bodies of the poor and oppressed peoples who are lacking a nation strong enough to defend against the dragon. Thus, it is a Jeremiad that speaks to us of an angry God who calls down judgment on the future. And yet, can we not also perceive its uncanny accuracy in providing a diagnosis of our contemporary moment, the image of a brother who returns to claim the "fire and fury" of an archaic father, who replaces the confidence in a revolutionary ideal of universal democratization with the *Realipolitik* of universal racism, who replaces the last traces of confidence and trust in a society without fathers with the hatred for the global poor, and the desire to murder the orphans and the widows of the world? As Rousseau said, "The strongest is never strong enough to be master all of the time, unless he transforms force into right." However, as Kant added, the very principle of right is contained in the possibility of a reciprocal constraint or coercion (*wechselseitigen Zwanges*). Without this reciprocity and legal constraint on absolute power, the sovereign often appears as a man without a state, a captain without a crew (a people), adrift and alone on his ship like a brigand or a rogue. If only for this reason, Trump appears more and more each day as a sovereign in search of "a people who is missing," even though this is not necessarily "the American people," but more like a mob, a gang, a ship of fools (even though, we are told, "They are very fine people!"). Recalling the allusion to Melville—which is not insignificant as a prophecy of "our sick America"—we can only hope that this motley crew is not doomed to perish from the earth along with their insane captain.

In the above prophetic account we can see a similar warning concerning the ideal of revolutions that can no longer count on the organic refashioning of the primitive nation into either a universal class or super-proletariat. In its place we have the universalization of the process of "becoming minor" that seems to transform only the poor and destitute masses who grow at the periphery of global capitalist society. Today, the failure of both revolutions is clear as day, or maybe as the night when all the cows are black. This is particularly true if we view the status of each universal: the universal fabricated by the creation of a "patchwork" of nations and ethnicities has been negated by the paternal function of one national race, by the dream of consanguinity and "America first"; by contrast, the communist idea of producing the new universal man and a scientific society of brothers has been overthrown by the return of the archaic Russian nation, the restored dream of sovereign particularism, and by a kind of grotesque return of either Peter the Great or Ivan the Terrible. Does the current situation of sovereignty present us with a third universal, one that replaces the messianic universals of the nineteenth century with the millenarian image of universal destitution?

At the conclusion of his jeremiad concerning the failure of the two great revolutionary societies, particularly the failure of the American revolution as foretold by the great nineteenth-century prophet, Herman Melville, Deleuze once again makes an immediate association to the situation of "small nations" as described earlier by Kafka:

> What Kafka would say about "small nations" is what Melville already said about the great American nation: it must become a patchwork of all small nations. What Kafka would say about minor literatures is what Melville had already said about the American literature of his time: because there are so few authors in America, and because the people are so indifferent, the writer is not in the position to succeed as a recognized master. *Even in his failure, the writer remains all the more bearer of collective enunciation and preserves the rights of a people to come, or of a human becoming.*[7]

In other words, here we see the reprisal of the three characteristics of the concept of minor literature that were drawn from Kafka's diaries of 1911: the scarcity of creators, the lack of a dominant paternal function of a master writer and a major tradition of literary history, and the open-ended possibility to develop in several future directions. As in the case of Deleuze and Guattari's earlier gloss of these characteristics, this is said to produce a "high co-efficient of deterritorialization" and a greater degree of collective enunciation.

I have already treated these three themes from the perspective of Kafka's situation as a writer of a "small nation." Moreover, I have called into question the central premise of Deleuze and Guattari's notion of the writer as bachelor, that is, as the solitary figure who bears the seeds of collective enunciation in the absence of the nation (i.e., who "preserves the rights of the people") and who thus functions in the present context as a "relay" in the circuit of the revolutionary becoming of the people. I will not continue to quibble over the details of this comparison, but simply point to the bizarre figure of Bartleby himself, who appears at the end of this sequence as a universal bachelor, who now assumes the "schizophrenic vocation" of the writer in a state of permanent and universal exile; thus, even in his failure as a relay to revolutionary becoming, he becomes nonetheless "the new Christ or the brother to us all."[8] In other words, Bartleby becomes a figure of a new universal "becoming minor," and it is precisely in his catatonic and anorexic state that *he so eloquently speaks "for all of us" when he says: "I would prefer not to."*

According to the book of Bartleby, at least as told by Deleuze, even in its failure the American revolution would continue to send out its fragments, until eventually the world itself becomes a patchwork of all "small nations." Ironically, this prophetic word echoes one possible future that was already foretold by Kant at the end of the eighteenth century in *Perpetual Peace* (1795) concerning the creation of what he called a *foidus pacificum* (confederacy of peaceful nations). However, Kant also warned that such a universal and cosmopolitan state-form—one that even surpasses the nineteenth-century idea of communism as a universal state—can never be realized until the eighteenth-century idea of the nation-state as such is abolished, since it is founded upon sovereignty and the right of war (*jus bellum*) to guarantee its future survival, while the cosmopolitan state is founded upon the perfection of international law and peaceful intercourse between a diversity of nations, not the creation of one race or sovereign people through revolutionary or absolute partisan warfare.[9] As we have already observed under the theme of the return of a paternal function, judging from recent events and sovereign personages we are witnessing instead a recon-solidation of earlier forms of the nation-state. Moreover, it is interesting to observe that the return of the paternal function of the nation is most remarkable in the three great revolutionary societies of the twentieth century: the United States, Russia, and China.

Before returning to the original sense of the refrain itself, finally, I wish to outline another possible destination of the politics of the nation-state: the one that appears in the writings of Hannah Arendt concerning the future of totalitarianism. As Arendt predicts in *The Origins of Totalitarianism*, "it may be that the true predicaments of our time will assume their authentic form . . . only when totalitarianism has become a thing of the past."[10] In other words, with the deaths of Stalin and Hitler, the fall of National Socialism and the collapse of the Soviet Union, the full phenomenon of fascism and totalitarianism is still not behind us, since its causes remain on our contemporary horizon. This is why Arendt's analysis of the causes of the historical phenomenon is so prescient for approaching our present-day situation, as her own definition of the current threat vacillates somewhere between a makeshift arrangement that emerges as the symptom of the crisis of a historical arrangement of the body politic (such as socialism or democracy, a pronounced crisis that is clearly pronounced in the American form of democracy today), on the one hand, or as a completely unprecedented and novel form of government, which we are only now beginning to see glimpses of in the unique combination of late capitalism and a centralized form of state control in China, on the other. In fact, the question Arendt poses is whether there is, strictly speaking, something like a single nature of a totalitarian govern- mentality that could be defined like other forms of government recognized by Western political traditions over the past two hundred years. It is in the line of such reflections to raise the question of whether totalitarian government, born of this crisis and at the same time its clearest and only unequivocal symptom, is merely a makeshift arrangement, which borrows its methods of intimidation, its means of organization, and its instruments of violence from the well-known political arsenal of tyranny, despotism, and dictatorships, and owes its existence only to the deplorable, but perhaps accidental, failure of the traditional political forces—liberal or conservative, national or socialist, republican or monarchist, authoritarian or democratic.[11]

If we examine only a few of the features of the earlier historical arrangement in order to apply them to our present context, first we can clearly see the return of a one-party system in several regions globally, which today might also characterize the reli- gious and political movements that have emerged alongside fundamentalist Islam and post-communist nations. Second, we find in all cases a sovereign defiance of positive law—especially those positive laws that determine the natural rights belonging to all individuals without regard to custom, tradition, nationality, race, or sex—often in the claim of a higher form of legitimacy, if not, as Arendt observed, a direct access to the source of the law itself to establish its "rule of justice" across the earth. Third, as a consequence of the above claim, in keeping with Kant's earlier warning today we still find a notion of "right" that can only be predicated on the right of war (*jus bellum*), as if war were an absolute necessity to guarantee the perpetuation of the biopolitical existence of a distinctive "people." In short, what Arendt constantly underlines as a novelty is a "monstrous" form of sovereign right (i.e., "justice") *without the need of either politics or legality*, both of which this sovereign believes he can do without, because he certainly does not need to concern himself with the consensus of his own subjects or with the positive laws that determine the rights of other national subjects, especially given the justification of war. "If it is true," Arendt wrote concerning the last century,

> that the link between totalitarian countries and the civilized world was broken through the monstrous crimes of totalitarian regimes, it is also true that this criminality was not due to simple aggressiveness, ruthlessness, warfare and treachery, but to a conscious break of that *consensus juris* which, according to Cicero, constitutes a "people," and which, as international law, in modern times has constituted the civilized world insofar as it remains the foundation-stone of international relations even under the conditions of war.[12]

Today, moreover, it is important to see that the monstrous crimes of the current century are committed not only by new totalitarian regimes, as in the case of Syria, but also by "non-state actors" in international territories where, just as in the case of civil war, there can be neither right nor wrong committed on either side without the reciprocal recognition of a common principle of civility (*consensus juris*). Even the democratic states themselves have abandoned this principle of consensus by employing use of drones and assassins in their relentless global pursuit of *an unknown and indeterminate enemy*, thus openly and routinely violating a major principle of international law as Kant outlined in the sixth preliminary article of *Perpetual Peace*: "No nation at war with another shall permit such acts of war as shall make mutual trust impossible during some future time of peace" (including the use of assassins, or *percussores*).[13] What we find among all these contemporary parties, in different respects and according to different measures, is the evidence of this conscious break with this principle of civil society that has extended from the last century and has only widened in the present one to engulf the entire planet. Thus, today the sovereign can still murder his own people, or minimally, the populations who dwell within the boundaries of the nation's territory; the terrorist networks can send their human drones into the crowded streets of London, Paris, Barcelona, and New York; likewise, the states themselves can deploy drones to indiscriminately target individuals in other territories without this act producing too strenuous a contraction in the principle of international law. Nevertheless, this still constitutes a contradiction within the idea of "right," which is founded upon nothing less than a permanent threat of violence (and which in our century continues to inform the real and permanent threat of nuclear war). Kant foresaw the nature of this contradiction at the end of the eighteenth century when he argued that the right to go to war is meaningless and cannot be properly conceived as a universally valid element in the rights of nations. "Consequently," Kant wrote, "the concept of the right of nations must be understood as follows: that it serves justly those men who are disposed to seek one another's destruction and thus to find perpetual peace in the grave that covers all the horrors of violence and its perpetrators."[14]

At this point I will return to the primary subject of my reflection, which is not the destination of the nation-state or the Kantian idea of universal cosmopolitanism but rather the concept of "minor literature" and its supposed connection to the statements concerning a missing or absent people. In fact, we still have not demonstrated this relationship, but I think I have demonstrated that Deleuze and Guattari haven't either, which is why the statement functions mechanically, in the manner of an axiom, as the cause of what they call the "literary machine." An axiom is a first statement or principle that does not require demonstration, because it must be assumed as a given for every proposition that follows and thus cannot be submitted to further analysis without threatening the logical consistency of the entire argument. In other words, the machine would break down. Accordingly, as a major axiom of their argument for a "minor literature," Deleuze and Guattari must assume *a priori* the connection between the writer determined as a bachelor and a collective assemblage of enunciation, determined as absent or missing. In this situation, "the literary machine thus becomes the relay for a revolutionary machine-to-come, not at all for ideological reasons but because the literary machine alone is determined to fill the conditions of a collective enunciation that is lacking elsewhere in this milieu: *literature is the people's concern*."[15] It is precisely the status of a collective assemblage of enunciation that is found to be either absent or missing elsewhere that will determine what literary enunciation provides in its place, which Deleuze and Guattari call a "relay" or a "connector" in a mechanical sense, almost in the sense of closing a circuit according to the machinic analogy they employ throughout the Kafka book, especially in the chapter "The Connectors."[16]

In fact, this missing relay or connector is only established later in *A Thousand Plateaus*, in "The Postulates of Linguistics," where they deny the existence of individual enunciation itself. As they write: "There is no individual enunciation. There is not even a subject of enunciation."[17] Thus, what is called individuated enunciation is actually only an instance or degree of collective enunciation. Once we accept this as an axiom, "it becomes clear that the statement is individuated, and the enunciation is subjectified, only to the extent that an impersonal collective assemblage requires it and determines it to be so."[18] In short, if the vital relay is missing, neither the writer nor the people can connect with one another in the form of a concrete assemblage (e.g., a nation); they remain in the state of an "open circuit." (In Bartleby's famous statement, "I would prefer not to," we are given the primary example of the nonfunctional relay of the open circuit between an individuated enunciation and a missing collective assemblage.) Moreover, the solitary writer who is anonymous and the people who are absent are suddenly found to share the same lack of recognition, or more precisely, lacking the means of producing their own objective form of recognition in social space. In fact, this lack becomes endemic and proliferates among the parties involved in the scene of recognition: the people do not recognize their own writers any more than they have the objective means to recognize themselves. Thus, the writer lacks a definite "public" and the official institutions of literary history; the people lack the political and legal means of recognition (i.e., a constitution, a state-form, positive law, etc.). In other words, although the people are not exactly anonymous, they nevertheless exist under the juridical determination of a "minor people."

As I recounted earlier with regard to the second sense of the refrain "the people are missing," which I translated from the French phrase literally and according to a nineteenth-century understanding of a minority as a "stateless people," it is interesting that Deleuze and Guattari choose to render the sense of *manqué* only to refer to conditions that are presumed to exist in a major language. Accordingly, literary enunciation alone is determined to fulfill these absent conditions of political recognition that are already presupposed by a major national literature. And yet, once again, this begs the question of how literary enunciation can be determined to fulfill the conditions of recognition assumed by the state, the courts, literary history, and so forth. If we recall Kafka's own description of the phrase "literature is a concern of the people," it is primarily determined in a minor setting by means of "political slogans." Could these also not function as relays to collective assemblages of enunciation? But how is this not caused by ideological reasons, and in what way can the "relay" between politics and literary activity not function ideologically, at least to some degree?

Once again, since Deleuze and Guattari derive their understanding of the connection between literature and minority politics almost entirely from the brief description given in the June 1911 journal entry, I will return to Kafka's own representation of this connection. First, I simply quote (in the manner of a list of attributes or traits) what Kafka defines as the benefits of literature for the Jews of Warsaw (drawn from Löwy's account) and the Czech people of Prague (from his own insights):

- the stirring of minds,
- the coherence of national consciousness, often unrealized in public life and always tending to disintegrate,
- the pride that a nation gains from a literature of its own and the support it is afforded in the face of a hostile surrounding world,
- this keeping a diary of the nation which is something entirely different from historiography and results in a rapid (and yet always closely scrutinized) development,
- the spiritualization of the broad area of public life,
- the assimilation of dissatisfied elements that are immediately put to use precisely in this sphere where only stagnation can do harm,
- the constant integration of a people with respect to its whole that the incessant bustle of the magazines creates [i.e., its "liveliness"],

- the narrowing down of the attention of the nation on itself and the accepting of what is foreign only in reflection,
- the birth of a respect for those active in literature,
- the transitory awakening in the younger generation of higher aspirations, which nevertheless leaves its permanent mark,
- the acknowledgment of literary events as objects of political solicitude,
- the dignification of the antithesis between fathers and sons and the possibility of discussing this,
- the presentation of national faults in a manner that is very painful, to be sure, but also liberating and deserving of forgiveness,
- the beginning of a lively and therefore self-respecting book trade and the eagerness for books.[19]

Even though literary history has labeled Kafka a tragic and pessimistic writer, I do not know a more positive, optimistic, and hopeful view of the benefits of literature for any nation, major or minor. However, it is clear that Kafka's prognosis only concerns a "small nation," a minority, a stateless people, whose political existence in the fullest sense is only an idea that belongs in the full development of a possible future, even though the natural development of literary culture is outlined in a manner that seems to assume this final destination is inevitable. Of course, there are obstacles and setbacks to this natural development, if not what Deleuze calls "the diabolical powers knocking at the door," and Kafka immediately addresses these in the observations that stem from his own experiences with the minor literary culture of Prague.

First, there is the problem of bias that is the seat of all petty polemics in any minor tradition: "Since people lack a sense of context, their literary activities are out of context too."[20] Moreover, this bias leads to prejudice and a tendency among the minor figures to place themselves above their equals (since "there is no writer of great talent whose great gifts could silence at least the majority of the cavaliers"), and it is in this climate of general insecurity and resentment between equals that the boundary of the political is reached. As I already observed, according to Kafka's astute prognosis of the culture of minorities, this "limiting boundary" is reached too early and is found to be everywhere, to the extent that the popular dissemination of literature occurs only on the basis of "political slogans." It is not by accident that this limiting boundary of politics continues to dominate the dissemination of minority literatures in the university, where the connection between literature and politics is often made on the same basis, and we must observe that the concept of "minor literature" itself has been disseminated throughout the North American university over the last forty years exactly in the manner of a "political slogan."

Kafka's sketch addresses a broad area of the benefits of literary culture and production, which is not narrowly telescoped on political interpretation of particular works and their authors, nor is it imminently connected to the idea of revolution as it is in Deleuze and Guattari's interpretation. Certainly, there is the seed of national consciousness as the very reason for all the benefits that seem to grow organically toward some natural destination in the form of the nation: the stimulation of minds, pride, greater national coherence, the spiritualization of public life, the clarification of intergenerational conflicts, the public discussion of painful history, and so forth. To conclude his observations on the total form of minority literary culture (before he returns again in the diary to the constant theme of circumcision), Kafka organizes all the benefits under three categories (liveliness, less constraint, popularity), and it is only under the last that the connection with politics appears:

a. Connection with politics.
b. Literary history.
c. Faith in literature, can make up their own laws.[21]

Following Kafka's own categories, we can see that in the natural development of the literature of a small nation the connection to politics comes last. It does not appear as a condition, as in Deleuze and Guattari's interpretation, nor is there any indication that the final growth of the nation will occur through revolutionary action. In fact, from this we can only conclude that Deleuze and Guattari's definition of minor literature best fits Kafka's earlier diagnosis, given in the diary, of the premature boundary of the political according to the second major characteristic: the connection of the individual to political immediacy, the tendency to find the political at the basis of every social relation (e.g., familial, bureaucratic, juridical), even before it is actually there (e.g., immanence).

On the other hand, according to Kafka's table, a small nation's faith in its own literary creativity eventually leads to the institution of its own literary history, and this naturally leads to a confidence in the creation of its own political and legal institutions. In other words, the natural development of the small nation's popular culture follows the same historical progression as seen in the larger established nations that Kafka addresses in his diary entry, especially the German culture of Goethe. It is clear that Kafka's views on the natural development of a popular and political culture of the people were influenced by the *Volksphilosophie* of Johann Gottfried Herder, especially his conception of the "people" (*Volk*) as the basis of an organic and independent spiritual nation, and for his prophetic belief that the Slavic peoples of eastern Europe would eventually unite to become the most powerful European culture, while the western European nations withered away under the influence of Christianity (i.e., nihilism). While I cannot develop this point any further in the space of these reflections, I would simply recall here that Kafka gave a public reading of his first story "The Judgment" for the recently founded Johann Gottfried Herder Association for the Promotion of Theoretical Interests on December 4, 1912, exactly one year after the diary of December 1911.

It is in the context of a natural philosophy of culture that I will now revise the second component of the refrain "the people are missing" by returning to the statement of Paul Klee that Deleuze often recites as his primary source. The passage is found in Klee's 1924 *Über moderne Kunst* (*On Modern Art*), the lecture given at his exhibition at the Kunstverein in Jena on January 26, 1924. At the conclusion of the talk in which Klee outlines the principles of his two methods to drawing and color, he says:

> Sometimes I dream of a work of very great breadth, ranging through the whole region of element, object, meaning, and style.

> This, I fear, will remain a dream, but it's a good thing even now to bear the possibility occasionally in mind.

> Nothing can be rushed. It must grow, it should grow of itself, and if the time ever comes for that work—so much the better!

> We must go on seeking it!
> We have found the parts, but not the whole!
> We still lack the ultimate power, for:
> the people are not with us.[22]

The last two lines enunciate a slightly different sense of the refrain, which could perhaps be very loosely translated as "the people are missing." The original German text reads: "Wir haben noch nicht diese letzte Kraft, denn: uns trägt kein Volk" (We do not yet have this last strength, because: no nation carries us). In the French version from which Deleuze's own reading is probably derived, the lines are rendered "Il nous manque cette dernier force. Faute d'un peuple qui nous porte" (We are missing this final force, for lack of a people who carries us). Once again, this introduces a notion of "lack" (*manque*) that appears in the French phrase *le peuple manqué*, but it also uses a metaphor of a force that will carry "us" (artists) as a great wind, which was first introduced by the critic Walter Benjamin in his description of Klee's *Angelus Novus* as being blown from behind by the great wind of history. At this point, however, I am only speculating on the source of this metaphor, which casts a revolutionary or messianic interpretation of the force that will complete the work of art.

On the other hand, Klee's own image of this force is the "whole" (*die Ganze*). It is the force of nature itself, to grow of itself, from its own power, and the people are identified with this force of nature that produces the complete artwork, giving it its "final cause." This image is given earlier in his lecture where Klee describes the complete elements of parts of the power of creation as a tree. The roots would be the elemental existence of the people in their language, their symbols, and their perceptions; the work of art would be the crown, and the artist himself is described as the trunk, whom Klee calls the "humble mediator." In other words, this last strength needed to complete the great work does not belong to the powers of the artist (or natural genius), who lacks sufficient strength, but rather to the nature of the nation or the people, depending on how one wants to render the German term *Volk*. Accordingly, the people Klee dreams of who will provide the strength to complete the great work of culture is not a revolutionary people, nor is it a minority or stateless people, and thus the power is not to be identified with the messianic force of history, according to Benjamin's figure of the Angel being blown backwards into eternity. On the contrary, Klee says, this final development must not be forced; rather, "it must grow of itself."

According to Klee's image of culture, therefore, the people are associated with the ultimate power that completes the great work of art. Without them, or if they are found to be absent in some manner, either lost or still waiting to be born, the artwork will remain unfinished and incomplete until a sufficient people become its true receivers, since they are the true cause of its creation. Until then, the artwork will exist only as a sketch of the future work, or perhaps it will remain unfinished for all eternity. Of course, this must remain a possibility too for the future of the artwork, whether individual or collective. Nevertheless, in a note of sober optimism that recalls the line from Kafka's diaries, or from his short fragment "Message from the Emperor," Klee confesses: "This, I fear, will remain a dream, but it's a good thing even now to bear the possibility occasionally in mind." We should also note that less than ten years later, Klee will lose his professorship in Düsseldorf under the sanction of the National Socialist takeover of the university. The self-portrait completed in the same year portrays the artist himself in dark colors and shows his closed eyes and compressed lips. On the back of his head there is a large X symbolizing that his art was no longer valued by the German *Volk* of his time.

Here, it is in Klee's own experience that we might locate the final sense of the refrain, which can no longer be translated from the French phrase without again introducing a foreign idea to represent the causality of art, or the mysterious source of schematism of the artwork and the complete idea of community. We have discovered this sense as well in the brief table that Kafka provides from his diary, partly a reflection on his own experience in Prague or on the theater of Löwy in the Warsaw ghetto, when he gives the nature of this force a very practical interpretation as merely a degree of "popularity" that is the visible sign of the people's reception of its own writers. Thus, the public sign of popularity initially leads to a feeling of pride in its own artists and writers, and eventually to the creation of its own cultural history and producing a kind of "faith" that speaks directly to the people's ability to create its own laws, that is, to become an independent and sovereign nation. Finally, it is only in this sense, which initially appears as a sign of recognition (even self-recognition), that the popularity of the culture of small nations is the seed of "the people to come" (i.e., if this natural development of force is allowed to grow of itself and is not interrupted or canceled out altogether by other forces that are external to the relationship between the writer and his or her people).

On the other hand, lacking this public sign of mutual recognition, according to which "literature is a concern of the people," the work itself falls into the shade of popular culture, and the artist or writer suffers an ambiguous and completely isolated existence. Is this not the very fate of literature or art after modernism? The work itself becomes a broken symbol, and the artist or writer's own identity is placed in question, becoming the anonymous name marked by an X in the imagination of a people who may (or may not) yet exist. As a result, the question concerning the relationship between the writer or artist and his or her people becomes the source of an entirely different concern, a form of suspicion and incredulity that substitutes criticism for art, and ultimately generates a feeling of resentment toward the creator herself. Moreover, is this not the fate of the artist and writer after the postmodern regime of "political interpretation"? Ultimately, one substitutes a feeling of betrayal for the feeling of pride in one's own literature, and in place of faith or optimism in the idea of the artwork we feel the dominant psychological and existential moods of doubt, fear, pessimism, equivocation, cynicism, self-loathing, and even self-hatred.

Most of all, in the departments of "LITERATURE" today there is an abiding suspicion and hatred of all creators! In other words, recalling the "divorce" of the practical understanding of the creative writer and the critical judgment of the political theorist or academic philosopher, which can now be employed analogically to represent the contemporary embodiment of the faculties, it is clear they no longer share a common object, and thus, there is no longer any consensus between them concerning what is the sense of the aesthetic presentation. In place of even a minimal consensus concerning the harmony of the two aspects of judgment (the knowledge or technique employed in the act of making, and the knowledge of form) there is only a "feeling" of an extreme *dissensus*, to invoke Rancière, or the sign of a *differend* between heterogeneous phrase universes, according to Lyotard's sense. Although some might complain I am being too allegorical in my figuration of these faculties by their historical representatives in the contemporary moment, we must remember that the Kantian invention of the term *faculty* itself is patently metaphorical in its historical representation of the mental faculties (or rather, mental powers) of imagining, reasoning, and understanding in a synthetic form that unifies the subjective and objective conditions of experience and intuition in one representation. These general powers are always already figured by their empirical-historical representatives, even in Kant, for whom the faculty of the imagination is portrayed by the conceptual personae of genius, and the philosopher assumes the role of the legislator in accordance with the ideas of reason. To picture the nature of this *differend* today, between the creator and the specialized critic (who is not "the public"), each party has become closed up in the immanent understanding of its own "idea," which has produced the kind of madness that today inflicts the development of contemporary art and literature.

Translating this development according to Klee's symbolic

image of the total idea of the artwork as a great tree, the people are the subterranean roots, the artist is the trunk (or "humble mediator"), and the artist's lifelong work is the crown of the tree. Following the logic of this natural symbol, if the roots become desiccated, the first sign of death is the browning of the crown and the loss of the needles from the top downward; eventually, all that remains is the bare and solitary trunk, like those huge monoliths of California pine that stand guard like sentinels along the Pacific Coast Highway. These lonely and dead pines could also symbolically represent the figures of great writers in a nation's literary history, or the solitary monoliths of modernist art. According to this representation, Kafka and Klee would merely be two dead and giant monoliths stuck in the dead and burned-out soil of postmodern culture, where there is no longer even the slightest trace of a people, either still missing or yet to come. Of course, all writers and critics know this feeling when they are honest enough to admit it, but perhaps only in the moments of quiet desperation and pain. Perhaps the only antidote to this pessimism and world-weariness can be found in Klee's own cautious and sober optimism in the statement above, which comes from the artist's failure and rejection by his own people. In other words, even though the final completion of the work will remain a dream, it is still a good thing even now to bear the possibility occasionally in mind. In the end, we can find the same cautious yet hopeful feeling in Deleuze's own final confession on the future of art as resistance to the present:

> The people are missing and at the same time they are not missing. The people are missing means that the fundamental affinity between a work of art and a people that does not yet exist is not, will never be clear. And yet, there is no work of art that does not call on a people who does not yet exist.[23]

Year 2021

Minor Literature Today

"The people are missing, and at the same time, they are not missing."[1] It seems, after a long evolution of the refrain, this is the ambiguous situation we face today, and the final sense of the refrain has the same tautological structure as this passage from Beckett: "It is midnight. The rain is beating on the windows. It was not midnight. It was not raining." I will conclude, therefore, by commenting on the statements on each side of this contemporary tautology of minor literature and minor cinema today.

First, concerning the people who are not missing, the long history of the antipathy of the left for actual peoples is well documented, beginning with the Frankfurt School's realization in the wake of National Socialism of the loss of the working class as an organic revolutionary subject. Deleuze's own sober assessment in 1985 was perhaps influenced by the same realization concerning the French working class in the post-Dirigiste climate of the 1980s. In Deleuze's case, however, the emphasis is upon this philosopher's own inability to identify with any people (with the possible exception of the Palestinians), but especially not with the disorganization of the European and American working classes. In fact, it was the tendency to organize themselves into either ethnic minorities or nationalist subgroups that made them fall prey to fascism, populism, tribalism, religious fanaticism, and racism. The Frankfurt School's earlier response was to conduct a sociological study of the working classes in Germany and the United States in all aspects of their group psychology in order to construct a scientific knowledge of their fascist tendencies. Marcuse reoriented the subject of the proletariat to the subaltern classes and races that existed in the periphery of liberal society globally. The other major response was to abandon any hope for an existing people or organic community and to instead appeal to the utopian image of the people who are yet to come, whether this prayer was colored by the language of Judaic messianism, as in the case of Benjamin, or, today, by a posthumanist and secular idea of the multitude. Still other alternatives have simply amounted to substituting for the actual social group an abstract entity such as a pure category of universal history (Althusser), the absolute subject of communism (Badiou), an empty category in hegemonic strategies (Laclau and Mouffe), a purely discursive function (Foucault), or a permanent aporia in the idea of transcendental subjectivity (Derrida, Nancy). As a result, today we have a Manichaean dichotomy between the missing people and peoples who exist: the people who are missing are often depicted as angels compared with the devils that exist. (It is not difficult to discern in these extremes the poisonous fruit of the idealism of the younger Marx that has set his children's teeth on edge.) In the end, what we are left with is either a cardboard or paper people, on the one hand, or the dream of those bright and angelic beings that we only encounter in science fiction, on the other.

Deleuze and Guattari are themselves part of a post-Marxist tradition that attempts to invent a new subject to replace the subject of the proletariat, or the organic being of the multitude, but their specific strategy is to supplant the being of the subject with an open-ended and transversal "process" of "becoming minor." Ironically, according to their own metaphor of a closed versus open circuit or connection in an assemblage of collective enunciation, as with any open circuit, the machine cannot work because it lacks any power. Perhaps this is one explanation for the decline of the literary machine as a symbol of the revolutionary conditions of struggle, and Deleuze's displacement of these same conditions to the cinema of the third world ten years later, and especially to the marginalized populations who henceforth are the only ones who now have the right to claim "the people are missing."

But who or what is the "people" being invoked by each sense of the refrain? A revolutionary people, a minority or ethnic people, a stateless or decolonized people, or simply the permanent site of the failure of any social group to realize the organic idea of community? In response to this question, Immanuel Wallerstein's 1988 observation is exceptional for clarifying this issue. As he concludes:

> For more than a hundred years, the world Left has bemoaned its dilemma that the world's workers have all too often organized themselves in "people" forms. But this is not a soluble dilemma. It derives from the contradictions of the system. There cannot be *für sich* class activity that is entirely divorced from people-based political activity. We see this in the so-called national liberation movements, in all the new social movements, in the anti-bureaucratic movements in socialist countries.
>
> Would it not make more sense to try to understand peoplehood for what it is—in no sense a primordial stable social reality, but a complex, clay-like historical product of the capitalist world-economy through which the antagonistic forces struggle with each other. We can never do away with peoplehood in this system nor relegate it to a minor role.

On the other hand, we must not be bemused by the virtues ascribed to it, or we shall be betrayed by the ways in which it legitimates the existing system.[2]

The nineteenth-century idea of the people as nation-state and the twentieth-century idea of the stateless people are not actually the same entities invoked in the final sense of the refrain. Throughout the course of my reflections on the entity of the "people," therefore, I have intentionally restricted the term to its nineteenth-century notion consistent with Kafka's own understanding, which was influenced by the ethnocentric philosophy of Herder. This is why I have called attention to the assumptions of the primacy of language, territory, and culture. For Kafka, at least, a minority was defined by the absence of a state-form and territorial location, that is, a distinctive political identity according to the nineteenth-century understanding of the nation-state. (I have also pointed out the sheer difference in the number of actual territories and nations between Kafka's time and our own, given that the large majority of sovereign states in the world today have been created since 1914, the number of which has increased from 56 to approximately 193.) As Wallerstein has also observed, "The states that are today members of the United Nations are all creations of the modern world-system. Most of them did not even exist either as names or as administrative units more than a century or two ago."[3] Moreover, states come before nations, and not the other way around: "It is debatable whether the idea of 'nation' as a communal sentiment can exist before the actual creation of the state-form that represents a people," even if the form of the state is administrative or colonial and the "people" in question are determined to be ethnic minorities.[4] Consequently, beginning in the nineteenth century the creation of national literatures was part of a worldwide nation-building project that primarily served the state or colonial administered territories by creating internally homogeneous populations, even though there could be one state and many ethnic cultures, as was the case after the breakup of the Austro-Hungarian Empire in 1918.

And yet, concerning the people who are missing, as Deleuze also claims, "There is no work of art that does not call on a people who do not yet exist."[5] Klee says it more directly: "We [artists] seek a people." Why? For what? Is it to bring the artist and the people into actual existence through the medium of the artwork? This is the modernist sense of the refrain I have been examining. However, I believe I have clearly demonstrated that the same conditions for a minor literature do not exist today as they might have fifty years ago, and then it seems only for a decade. Concerning whether "LITERATURE" still exists today is an open question, and perhaps what Hegel predicted two hundred years ago about the death of the spirit of the artwork has finally come to pass. Despite the inherent pessimism of my claims, one thing is certain: the idea itself that lies at the condition of art still remains possible albeit unrealized—and perhaps unrealizable!—and even despite the decline of a particular historical genre or medium, such as literature or painting today. Thus, the idea of art, and its correlative, the idea of the people "as a great work of vast scope," can only exist today as a sketch or an unfinished novel. Perhaps both will remain incomplete, fragmentary, primitive, and unfinished. Concerning the hope of their final achievement we only have Klee's statement to console us, "It is a good thing even now to bear this possibility occasionally in mind."[6] In other words, *the essential purpose of the refrain is to express this feeling of incompleteness of the modern artwork by way of analogy.* It is not meant to refer to an existing people, but to the power of completeness that belongs to both the artwork and politics by means of an analogy; by means of this particular modern analogy, the people can conceive of their own completeness as the completion of art as a great work, as a *Bildungsroman* in which they are the protagonist. Kant understood this first, and Hegel only followed Kant's earlier intuition by recasting the entire history of philosophy into a *Bildungsroman*.

All political interpretation consciously or unconsciously ascribes to the artwork a certain power that directly invokes the existence of a people, particularly when the people are missing or yet to come. What is this power? Here, I will return to Kant and simply say that it is the capacity of having ideas. Deleuze also invokes this point when he defines an idea in cinema or literature as opposed to ideas in philosophy, or to ideas in general. Ideas in general—what Kant calls ideas of reason, or what Spinoza calls common notions—do exist as concepts without intuition. Ideas of art, or aesthetic ideas, actually do not exist in the same way. Rather, they emerge spontaneously from the work of art, and we lack any definite concepts to understand them. Nevertheless, the definite power of "having an idea" is what an "act" of art expresses, which is not limited to this or that particular idea that the artwork conveys as an image (whether linguistic, pictorial, or sonorous). When it becomes actual, the power of having an idea becomes a capacity, or what Kant called "a special faculty" that belongs to anyone who is also "susceptible" to having the same idea. Of course, Kant points to the sublime as only most extreme example of being susceptible to ideas, even though this susceptibility is described as a particular sensitivity to ideas that do not emerge from either perception or understanding, and this causes pain to all the other faculties. The imagination can conceive of these ideas only negatively, and what this experience communicates to the other faculties (or powers) is a feeling of pain, or rather impotence, a loss of power or capacity to actualize the idea in experience. We can also compare this experience to the feeling that Klee expresses when he can imagine the final end of his great work, but immediately also expresses as a source of pain, sadness, depression, the lack of power to complete this work, to actualize the idea he has imagined.

Therefore, what is called an "idea" in art, as opposed to an idea in philosophy, has a precarious existence. Klee described it as existing when the artist has the power to imagine the idea of a great work but is still found be lacking the force to actualize it. It is at this point that Klee identifies a people with this final force that completes the work by giving it an existence that is more than the idea imagined by the artist. For the work to actually exist—that is, to be more than mere imagination—it requires first of all a power that is equal to the artist or writer's own capacity to have the same, if not identical, idea. Thus, the artist (or creator) is the first to have this capacity for having an idea, but the idea does not actually exist as a "work" until this initial capacity encounters a second power. It is this power that Klee identifies with a people, and Kant with "culture." As Kant said, "The aptitude of a people for any end that may bring happiness (such as freedom) can only be produced by its culture" (KU: 299). It is for this reason that Kant places what he calls "fine art," as distinguished from the mechanical or technical arts, as the final end according to the teleological plan of culture. Thus, it is only when two powers encounter each other in a work that the idea has actual existence. Prior to this encounter, both powers remain fundamentally unfulfilled, incomplete. The power of the artist or writer is relegated to sterile imagination and anonymity, and the particular culture of a people may have the capacity to have ideas in general yet be without works in which to recognize this capacity as their own unique power. Thus, every artwork carries within its own act an image of the end of the artwork itself. The genetic idea of the artist or writer must merge with the objective idea of the people who must recognize it as their own idea, and the power of imagination must belong equally to the writer and his or her public as a mutual power to conceive the idea as if belonging to the native power of the same subject. Kafka adds to this thematic of right by saying that the pride and confidence that a minor people feel in works of their own culture prepares the way for the confidence to create their own laws, or in the Kantian sense, to become self-legislating subjects, no longer subjugated by an external authority to the status of a being a minority.

As we have already seen in Klee, this theme of incompletion and failure to finish the work is a primary characteristic of Kafka's oeuvre as well. In short, Kafka's novels are failed works when judged from the standard of literary forms that are derived from major literatures. Kafka never finished anything. Was this his own failure as an artist, or is this in fact the fundamental trait of a minor work, as in the statement by Klee, such that the force of resistance which causes the work to remain in a miserable state of incompletion can be recognized as a collective problem? For example, what would it mean if Kafka actually completed the novels? According to what standard of literary form would we judge them to be finished, complete? This is something that Guattari directly addresses in a very late comment on Kafka's process, in which he corrects the teleological plan of the components of expression that he understood ten years earlier with Deleuze: "One would completely miss 'the Kafka effect,' in its actual instance and vitality," Guattari writes, "if one falls prey to a retrospective illusion by apprehending all the components of expression—i.e., the stories, the novels, the letters, the diaries—as totalities that are only partially achieved, as if they also exist as works that could be achieved in other circumstances had the author been able to complete them."[7] Instead, in the 1984 commentary, Guattari sees a constant evolution of a process that leads to an "open oeuvre," in which the forces of incompletion are due to the asemiotic nature of the assemblage that Kafka's process of deterritorialization engenders the primary and unconscious processes directly. "It is precisely this fundamental incompletion, this chronic precariousness that confers the processual dimension of Kafkaism, its power of open analysis, that tears it away from all 20th century literature."[8]

Concluding my meditation on the question of minor literature today, this end of culture I have invoked in place of an existing people is most pronounced in so-called political works of art, but the one who imagines it is not the artist (or creator) but rather the modern critic who misunderstands it as a social demand to be directed to the artist or the work itself. Moreover, this demand has assumed an overtly juridical form in which the work and the artist or writer is placed on trial for adhering to the criteria of political interpretation that are first established by the critics themselves. Thus, criticism has long assumed the form of a historical tribunal, and many artists and writers—especially "minority writers"—have failed to measure up to the demands that the critics have placed on them, even though the evidence against them is almost always circumstantial. It is truly Kafaesque, moreover, that the trial against the artist has never ended with a definite verdict of guilt or innocence, but only an indefinite adjournment, that is, until the trial begins again in a new court and before a new tribunal. It is only the critic who has the right to assign the end of culture, who assumes the political and theological role in the drama of final judgment. In order to liberate the concept of "minor literature" again, in my view we may have no other choice: first, we must kill all the critics; and second, we must close all the creative writing factories.

I realize, of course, that what I am saying bears the same scorn for certain kinds of criticism that first motivated Deleuze and Guattari's creation of the concept of minor literature (i.e., the hatred for the language of all presumed masters), provided we understand this concept as Deleuze and Guattari originally proposed it by saying that "minor no longer designates specific literatures but the revolutionary conditions for every literature within the heart of what is called great (or established) literature."[9] In other words, contrary to the modern tradition of political interpretation, it is only by first understanding the conditions of "becoming minor" that innately belong to any artwork or any literature that one can establish the criteria for defining popular literature, a marginal literature, or a minority literature, and not the other way around. In other words, what Deleuze calls the "creative act" that establishes the passage to the "collective assemblage of enunciation" cannot be imposed from outside the act of creation itself. In some ways, which I cannot expand on here, Deleuze and Guattari's argument bears a striking similarity to Adorno's theory of autonomous art, and it is not by accident that both Kafka and Beckett are also the primary exemplars. "The work of art does not have an end; there we agree with Kant," Adorno wrote in the 1962 reflection "Commitment," "but the reason is that it is an end."[10]

Nevertheless, as I have argued throughout, Deleuze and Guattari are more than a little precipitous in establishing the conditions of the act by denying the *fact* of individual enunciation in their axiom that *there are only collective assemblages of enunciation*. If I have telescoped my reading of Deleuze and Guattari's entire argument upon one page, this is because it is precisely it is here that they perform a leap of interpretation that is just as rhetorically artful as it is logically precipitous. However, it is precisely by means of this leap over the subject that they are suddenly able to resolve the entire dilemma of "mediation" that has preoccupied the tradition of Marxist aesthetic criticism for more than a hundred years. Essentially, they solve the problem by skipping a step in the equation, thus avoiding the need for any dialectical mediation between the individual and the collective. It is only by means of this leap that they can establish the exemplary position of the bachelor as an "agent that becomes all the more collective because an individual is locked into it in his or her solitude (it is only in connection to a subject that something individual would be separable from the collective)."[11] On the other hand, if there isn't a subject, then there is no way of connecting enunciation to the private and separate existence of the individual; therefore, every enunciation suddenly acquires a collective significance.

I have to confess that I have great admiration for Deleuze and Guattari's remarkable "gesture" (in the strongest sense) that attempts to cut the Gordian knot of all political interpretation, and it is regrettable that most of their readers have failed to apply their concept rigorously enough to all literature and not only the works written by minorities, thus reattaching the category of the subject as "the connector" in the relay to collective enunciation. Of course, there is more than a little irony in the fact that Deleuze and Guattari would never have imagined—not in 1975, at least—that their little manifesto against Marxist and psychoanalytic interpretations of Kafka in France would first find a home in the English departments of the United States in order to establish an official program of political interpretation. It is too bad that most critics did not get beyond the page I have highlighted and now read as the last cautionary statement in reply to the question "What Is Minor Literature?":

> How many styles or genres or literary movements, even very small ones, have only one single dream: to assume a major function in language, to offer themselves as a sort of state language, an official language. . . . Create the opposite dream: know how to create a becoming-minor.[12]

I will not speculate further on what the opposite dream might have looked like in place of the nightmare of the political interpretation of literature and culture that we have inherited over the past fifty years. As Deleuze once said about living in someone else's dreams, "What other people dream is very dangerous. Dreams are a terrifying will to power. Each of us is more or less the victim of other people's dreams."[13]

NOTES

1. THE AXIOM

1. Gilles Deleuze, *Cinema 2: The Time-Image*, trans. Hugh Tomlinson and Robert Galeta (London: Athlone Press, 1989), 219–20.
2. Deleuze, *Cinema 2*, 220.
3. Paul Klee, *Théorie de l'art moderne*, ed. and trans. Pierre-Henri Gonthier (Paris: Éditions Denoël/Gonthier, 1980), 33. My translation.
4. Gilles Deleuze and Félix Guattari, *Kafka: Toward a Minor Literature*, trans. Dana Polan (Minneapolis: University of Minnesota Press, 1986), 16.
5. Deleuze and Guattari, *Kafka*, 17 (emphasis added).
6. Stanley Corngold, "Kafka and the Dialectic of Minor Literature," *College Literature* 21, no. 1 (February 1994): 96.
7. Franz Kafka, *Diaries, 1910–1913*, ed. Max Brod (New York: Schocken Books, 1948), 194 (emphasis added).
8. Corngold, "Kafka and the Dialectic of Minor Literature," 96 (my emphasis).
9. Klaus Wagenbach, *Kafka's Prague: A Travel Reader*, trans. Shaun Whiteside (New York: Overlook Press), 111–13.

2. THE PRINCIPLE

1. Gilles Deleuze and Félix Guattari, *Kafka: Toward a Minor Literature*, trans. Dana Polan (Minneapolis: University of Minnesota Press, 1986), 29.
2. Franz Kafka, *Letters to Milena*, trans. Tania and James Stern (New York: Schocken Books, 1953), 9.

3. Dimitris Vardoulakis, *Freedom from the Free Will: On Kafka's Laughter* (Albany: SUNY Press, 2016), 19.

4. Franz Kafka, *Letters to Felice*, ed. Erich Heller and Jurgen Born, trans. James Stern and Elisabeth Duckworth (New York: Schocken Books, 1967), 156.

5. Emmanuel Levinas, *Totality and Infinity: An Essay on Exteriority*, trans. Alphonse Lingis (Pittsburgh: Duquesne University Press, 1969), 263.

6. Levinas, *Totality and Infinity*, 263.

7. Franz Kafka, *Diaries, 1910–1913*, ed. Max Brod (New York: Schocken Books, 1948), 324.

8. Franz Kafka, *Diaries, 1914–1923*, ed. Max Brod (New York: Schocken Books, 1949), 182.

9. Kafka, *Diaries, 1914–1923*, 183.

10. Kafka, *Diaries, 1914–1923*, 186.

11. Kafka, *Diaries, 1914–1923*, 190.

12. Kafka, *Letters to Felice*, 372.

13. Kafka, *Diaries, 1914–1923*, 201.

14. Franz Kafka, *The Complete Stories* (New York: Schocken Books, 1946), 220. I have also consulted Ian Johnston's translation from the 2007 ebook edition of *Classics Unbound*.

15. Kafka, *The Complete Stories*, 221.

16. Kafka, *The Complete Stories*, 220.

17. Franz Kafka, *The Trial* (New York: Schocken Books, 1968), 1.

18. Kafka, *The Complete Stories*, 5.

19. Kafka, *The Complete Stories*, 63.

20. Kafka, *The Complete Stories*, 67.

21. Kafka, *The Complete Stories*, 65.

22. Deleuze and Guattari, *Kafka*, 22.

23. Deleuze and Guattari, *Kafka*, 38.

3. THE TAUTOLOGY

1. Franz Kafka, *Diaries, 1910–1913*, ed. Max Brod (New York: Schocken Books, 1948), 192.

2. Stanley Corngold, "Kafka and the Dialectic of Minor Literature," *College Literature* 21, no. 1 (Feb. 1994): 94.

3. Kafka, *Diaries, 1910–13*, 197.

4. Corngold, "Kafka and the Dialectic of Minor Literature," 95.

5. Nicholas Thoburn, "The People Are Missing: Cramped Spaces, Social Relations, and the Mediators of Politics," *International Journal of Politics, Cult Soc* 29 (2016): 377.

6. Fredric Jameson, *A Singular Modernity: Essay on the Ontology of the Present* (London: Verso, 2002), 199–200.

7. Michaela Fišerová, "Kafka zvířetem, zvíře Kafkou: Deleuze a Derrida o literární animalitě," in *Gilles Deleuze o literatuře: Mezi uměním, animalitou a politikou*, by Michaela Fišerová, Martin Charvát, and Gregg Lambert (Praha: Togga, 2018), 122. Fišerová's translation.

8. Gilles Deleuze and Félix Guattari, *Kafka: Toward a Minor Literature*, trans. Dana Polan (Minneapolis: University of Minnesota Press, 1986), 55.

9. Jacques Rancière, *The Politics of Aesthetics*, trans. Gabriel Rockhill (London: Continuum, 2004), 47.

10. Jacques Rancière, *Dissensus: On Politics and Aesthetics*, trans. Steven Corcoran (New York: Continuum, 2010), 179.

11. Maryvonne Saison, "The People Are Missing," *Contemporary Aesthetics* 6 (2008), https://digitalcommons.risd.edu/cgi/viewcontent .cgi?article=1136&context=liberalarts_contempaesthetics.

12. Rancière, *Dissensus*, 179.

13. Saison, "The People Are Missing."

14. Rancière, *Dissensus*, 92.

15. Rancière, *Dissensus*, 189.

16. Roland Barthes, *The Rustle of Language*, trans. Richard Howard (Berkeley: University of California Press, 1984), 22.

17. Kafka, *Diaries, 1910–1913*, 149.

18. Corngold, "Kafka and the Dialectic of Minor Literature," 92.

19. Michaela Fišerová, *Partager le visible: Repenser Foucault* (Paris: L'Harmattan, 2013), 217–18. Fišerová's translation.

4. THE ETHICAL DUTY

1. Jacques Rancière, *The Politics of Aesthetics*, trans. Gabriel Rockhill (London: Continuum, 2004), 45.

2. Gilles Deleuze, *Cinema 2: The Time-Image*, trans. Hugh Tomlinson and Robert Galeta (London: Athlone Press, 1989), 219–20.

3. Deleuze, *Cinema 2*, 217.

4. Deleuze, *Cinema 2*, 217.

5. Deleuze, *Cinema 2*, 219.

6. Maryvonne Saison, "The People Are Missing," *Contemporary Aesthetics* 6 (2008), https://digitalcommons.risd.edu/cgi/viewcontent .cgi?article=1136&context=liberalarts_contempaesthetics (emphasis added).

7. Deleuze, *Cinema 2*, 224.

5. THE MORAL ANALOGY

1. Gilles Deleuze, *Cinema 2: The Time-Image*, trans. Hugh Tomlinson and Robert Galeta (London: Athlone Press, 1989), 217.

2. Gilles Deleuze, *Two Regimes of Madness: Texts and Interviews, 1975–1995*, ed. David Lapoujade, trans. Ames Hodges and Mike Taormine (Paris: Éditions de Minuit, 2003), 322–33.

3. Gilles Deleuze, *Two Regimes of Madness*, 327–28.

4. Jean-François Lyotard, *The Differend: Phrases in Dispute*, trans. Georges Van Den Abbelele (Minneapolis: University of Minnesota Press, 1988), 123.

5. Deleuze, *Two Regimes of Madness*, 328–29.

6. Deleuze, *Two Regimes of Madness*, 329.

7. Deleuze, *Two Regimes of Madness*, 323.

8. Lyotard, *The Differend*, 121.

9. Lyotard, *The Differend*, 121.

10. Lyotard, *The Differend*, 121.

11. Immanuel Kant, *Critique of the Power of Judgment*, trans. Paul Guyer and Erich Matthews (Cambridge: Cambridge University Press, 2002), 222. All parenthetical references will be shortened to KU.

12. Lyotard, *The Differend*, 168.

13. Immanuel Kant, *Critique of Pure Reason*, trans. Paul Guyer and Allen Wood (Cambridge: Cambridge University Press, 1998). All parenthetical references are to the A and B pagination of the first and second editions.

14. Samantha Matherne, "Kant and the Art of Schematism," *Kantian Review* 19, no. 2 (2014): 188. Lyotard also criticizes the basis of the analogy between pure (or transcendental) schematism and the plastic arts. See Lyotard, *The Differend*, 133.

15. Matherne, "Kant and the Art of Schematism," 183–84, 187–88.

16. Matherne, "Kant and the Art of Schematism," 192.

17. Lyotard, *The Differend*, 168.

18. Lyotard, *The Differend*, 132.

19. Lyotard, *The Differend*, 133.

20. Lyotard, *The Differend*, 133.

21. Matherne, "Kant and the Art of Schematism," 188.

22. Deleuze, *Difference and Repetition*, trans. Paul Patton (New York: Columbia University Press, 1994), 331–32.

23. Deleuze, *Difference and Repetition*, 132.

24. Gilles Deleuze, *Kant's Critical Philosophy*, trans. Hugh Tomlinson and Barbara Habberjam (Minneapolis: University of Minnesota Press, 1984), 49.

25. Deleuze, *Kant's Critical Philosophy*, 52.

26. Deleuze, *Kant's Critical Philosophy*, xii.

27. Deleuze, *Difference and Repetition*, 208.

28. Gilles Deleuze and Félix Guattari, *What Is Philosophy?* trans. Hugh Tomlinson and Graham Burchell (New York: Columbia University Press, 1994), 169.

29. Deleuze, *Kant's Critical Philosophy*, 52.

30. See Matherne, "Kant and the Art of Schematism," 196.

31. Matherne, "Kant and the Art of Schematism," 185.

32. Deleuze and Guattari, *What Is Philosophy?* 197.

33. Deleuze, *Two Regimes of Madness*, 315–16.

34. Deleuze, *Kant's Critical Philosophy*, 57.

35. Deleuze and Guattari, *What Is Philosophy?* 172.

36. Deleuze and Guattari, *What Is Philosophy?* 172.

37. Lyotard, *The Differend*, 168.

38. See Gregg Lambert, *Philosophy after Friendship: Deleuze's Conceptual Personae* (Minneapolis: University of Minnesota Press, 2017), 119–36.

39. Deleuze and Guattari, *What Is Philosophy?* 108.

40. Deleuze and Guattari, *What Is Philosophy?* 112.

6. THE FINAL REFRAIN

1. See Stephen Jay Gould, *Questioning the Millennium: A Rationalist's Guide to a Precisely Arbitrary Countdown* (New York: Harmony Books, 1997), 112.

2. Gilles Deleuze, *Essays Critical and Clinical*, trans. Daniel W. Smith and Michael Greco (Minneapolis: University of Minnesota Press, 1997), 84.

3. See Gregg Lambert, *Philosophy after Friendship: Deleuze's Conceptual Personae* (Minneapolis: University of Minnesota Press, 2017), 119–36.

4. Deleuze, *Essays Critical and Clinical*, 88.

5. Deleuze, *Essays Critical and Clinical*, 89.

6. Deleuze, *Essays Critical and Clinical*, 89.

7. Deleuze, *Essays Critical and Clinical*, 89–90 (my emphasis).

8. Deleuze, *Essays Critical and Clinical*, 90.

9. See Lambert, *Philosophy after Friendship*, 137ff.

10. Hannah Arendt, *The Origins of Totalitarianism* (New York: Mariner Books, 1973), 460.

11. Arendt, *The Origins of Totalitarianism*, 461.

12. Arendt, *The Origins of Totalitarianism*, 462.

13. Immanuel Kant, *Perpetual Peace and Other Essays*, trans. Ted Humphrey (London: Hackett, 1983), 109.

14. Kant, *Perpetual Peace*, 117.

15. Gilles Deleuze and Félix Guattari, *Kafka: Toward a Minor Literature*, trans. Dana Polan (Minneapolis: University of Minnesota Press, 1986), 17–18.

16. Deleuze and Guattari, *Kafka*, 63–71.

17. Gilles Deleuze and Félix Guattari, *A Thousand Plateaus*, trans. Brian Massumi (London: Continuum Books, 1987), 79.

18. Deleuze and Guattari, *A Thousand Plateaus*, 80.

19. Franz Kafka, *Diaries, 1910–1913*, ed. Max Brod (New York: Schocken Books, 1948), 191–92.

20. Kafka, *Diaries, 1910–1913*, 194.

21. Kafka, *Diaries, 1910–1913*, 195.

22. Paul Klee, *On Modern Art*, trans. Paul Findlay (New York: Faber and Faber, 1948), 54–55.

23. Gilles Deleuze, *Two Regimes of Madness: Texts and Interviews, 1975–1995*, ed. David Lapoujade, trans. Ames Hodges and Mike Taormine (Paris: Éditions de Minuit, 2003), 329.

1. Gilles Deleuze, *Two Regimes of Madness, Texts and Interviews, 1975–1995*, ed. David Lapoujade, trans. Ames Hodges and Mike Taormine (Paris: Éditions de Minuit, 2003), 324.

2. Etienne Balibar and Immanuel Wallerstein, *Race, Nation, Class: Ambiguous Identities*, trans. Chris Turner (London: Verso Press, 1991), 85.

3. Balibar and Wallerstein, *Race, Nation, Class*, 80.

4. Balibar and Wallerstein, *Race, Nation, Class*, 81.

5. Deleuze, *Two Regimes of Madness*, 324.

6. Paul Klee, *On Modern Art*, trans. Paul Findlay (New York: Faber and Faber, 1948), 54.

7. Félix Guattari, *Les années d'hiver, 1980–1985* (Paris: Bernard Barrault, 1986), 265–66. My translation.

8. Guattari, *Les années d'hiver*, 266.

9. Gilles Deleuze and Félix Guattari, *Kafka: Toward a Minor Literature*, trans. Dana Polan (Minneapolis: University of Minnesota Press, 1986), 18.

10. Theodore Adorno, "Commitment," *The Adorno Reader*, ed. B. O'Connor (Oxford: Blackwell, 2000), 32.

11. Deleuze and Guattari, *Kafka*, 18.

12. Deleuze and Guattari, *Kafka*, 27.

13. Deleuze, *Two Regimes of Madness*, 318.

To order or obtain more information on these or other University of
Nebraska Press titles, visit nebraskapress.unl.edu.

Ingram Content Group UK Ltd.
Milton Keynes UK
UKHW010656240323
418962UK00017B/658